Living Out Your God-Given Potential

Patrick J Dailey

Author

Living Out Your
God-Given Potential

To my wife, my family, friends, and to my son, Aaron. May you seek the deeper things of God.

CONTENTS

CONTENTS

Introduction

Thank you for reaching for this book. Within it lies some discoveries and information that I have come across that have helped me reach my God-given potential. In the same way that I have been helped, motivated, and inspired, it is my prayer that you too will be inspired. By picking up this book and absorbing the words you have begun your own journey. I am a firm believer that when you are on a path of continual learning and growth, you should share the knowledge, wisdom, and the information with others. You would be surprised how often you will learn more by teaching and sharing what you know.

I am not a theologian. This book is not made as an advanced manual for life. This book is not written to confuse you. This book was intentionally meant as a dialogue. This book was meant to be read like a conversation, warm and intimate. This book was not written to be cold, distant and a bore. This book was written for the common person, to the Christian, and to people who want to reach their God-given potential. This book was made to be an easy read. To me, simplicity matters. I desire that you who are reading this, improve one way or another. May you seek the deeper things of God. May you grow. This book was meant to be written as an authentic piece. I am doing my best to be as open and as real as possible.

My journey began back in late 2017. I had reached a point in my life most people would describe as, "making it". I had fallen and bought into the illusion of success. I will go into more detail about the illusion of success later. To simply put it, many of us are fed the illusion that we will find fulfillment in money, success, material things, and other endeavors. We are made for more than the shallowness that is prevalent in our world.

I thought I had made it. I was newly married and working in corporate America. I was making good money. I was comfortable. I had a stable position. I had gone to college, worked hard, and took my life to the next season: work and marriage. Ecclesiastes 3 clearly states that there exists a time and a season for everything. During that time, I felt that I had done everything that I was supposed to. I felt that life was this continual checklist of things that you have to do. Once I was out of high school, the first box was checked. Once I was in college, I was embarking on a new chapter of my life- the next box to be checked.

Looking back at it all, I realized that this type of mindset was an unhealthy mindset to have. It is easy to imagine that once you check off one of the boxes on the checklist, you move on to the next and proceed down the line. It seems to me that any person who lives like this will feel empty and incomplete.

I felt that I had arrived at the place where I wanted to be - at least that's what I thought. I thought I had it all, but why did I feel incomplete and unfulfilled? I asked myself,

"Isn't this the kind of success people want?"

Despite all this success I had achieved, a feeling of

emptiness endured. I was unsure. I was newly married, in debt, had some past hurt, I was trying to fit into a mold - I could go on and on. What was it? Was I stressed? Over-whelmed?

As humans, we are conditioned to fear change. We are creatures of habit. We typically like things to be the same. Change means new beginnings, a different outcome. - and that doesn't always guarantee what we hope for. We keep trying. We keep moving forward. Think about it - aren't we conditioned to: go to school, get good grades, graduate, and get a stable job that we work at for thirty-five years?

How could the way that I was raised to be wrong? Many people were doing it this way. I knew many of my friends, and peers who lived this way. These people went to college, got a job, and had the appearance that they were happy.

A few years back, I had seen a therapist who told me once, "If it's not working, try something else!" That's ex-actly what I needed.

Accepting that I needed to change was exactly what was needed in my life. It has been said that to have a different output, you need to have different input. During that time, I felt empty and that my life was made for more. I could either keep going on the trajectory that I was or do some-thing about it and change. This led me to the first step of realizing that I was made for more. I was put on Earth for a greater purpose and I believe you are as well.

To this day, I still believe that we are all made for a greater purpose. We are all made in the image of God, and we are all given different gifts and abilities that we need to decide to use or neglect.

I first had to acknowledge that something was missing. I was safe and secure with my position at work, yet I was lacking fulfillment and satisfaction. I was on a path of success, but not fulfillment. Surely, a lot of people say that they are happy and fulfilled, but they are not. It makes me think that many people out there will sacrifice their happiness, joy, and fulfillment in the name of the mighty dollar. People will trade their freedom for security and you will see this pattern happen often.

I was successful bust not fulfilled. I had changed positions and had gotten raises, and that was cool. What a rut! I technically had a career and a decent life, but at what cost? Matthew 16:26 CSB "For what will it benefit someone if he gains the whole world yet loses his life? Or what will anyone give in exchange for his life?" I have heard this verse many times before, and I was reminded of this verse from the pages of Scripture. Is it right for someone to sell out in the name of making it? Certainly, there had to have been another way.

One woman in particular at my work would constantly talk about how she had been doing the same thing for years. This was not a bad thing in her eyes in fact she made it know that doing the same thing day after day excited her. I lacked a mutual feeling. Was something wrong with me? I mean, if she was happy and fulfilled doing what she was doing every day, more power to her! In the same way, if you are completely happy doing what you are doing in life, I commend you. But I know, in my own circumstance, this was not the case.

"Only a few more years of this." "Only a few more days until Friday." "Thank God it's Friday!" These words spilled out mindlessly from the mouths of both myself and many co-workers. I constantly asked myself, "Is this really what my life has come to - or is there more to this?" How could someone be happy with this?

One day it hit me- I needed to observe the good and the bad. Some of my colleagues were actually happy, while a significant amount of others were unhappy. I began to pay more attention to those who were clearly miserable because of their current situations. What if many people bought into this? I wondered, how many people thought this way?

I came to the conclusion that a lot of people are living life in such a way where they are not happy or fulfilled. Some people accept it. Others are unaware. Some need motivation others will decline any other opinion. To these people, I dedicate this book. If you are unhappy in your current state, in your career, and where you are at in life, please consider reading this book. I wrote this book as a way to help inspire you to reach your God-given potential.

I feared change, I feared becoming like the individuals I was surrounded by. Their intense fear of change is what kept them there, feeling on edge. The fear that I had was the fear of settling for less than I was capable of. I had worked hard in college, I had a lot of people encouraging me and pushing me to graduate and to make something of myself. But I had learned that education does not mean that you are gifted or intelligent. I believe that education is merely a title. There is more than one way to measure a person's intelligence. Some other qualities to consider are character, talents, abilities, and certainly their successes. Education is one piece of the puzzle.

I believed that to change my output, I needed to change my input. Each day that I remained at corporate, I read books, took courses, and listened to audiobooks. I was educated, but I was in debt. As my therapist once told me, "If what you have done no longer works, it is time for a change." I originally was looking into more formal education, but at what cost. Instead of continuing on the path and journey of formal education, I had felt the urge to seek knowledge, information, and wisdom. I wagered that I could read the finest books, courses, and audio recordings from the most successful people in their field, and learn how they did it! To this day, I am still learning and growing, because I believe that education is a process rather than a checkbox.

I poured much of my time and effort into learning and growing before I decided to leave my job. I had this desire to go from where I was to where I wanted to be. Are many people unhappy? I talked to people who were working the typical nine-to-five job. The answers that I received varied greatly.

I wanted answers. Not all coworkers were unhappy, some were happy. I wished to know why some co-workers stayed despite being unhappy. What was initially a mild curiosity of mine, resulted in a deeper understanding of people.

There was one woman in my place of work that completely loved her job. I appreciated hearing this. It allowed me to recognize that different people are meant for different things in life. What remained was that I am on a different path - this job would eventually end and lead me elsewhere. This woman partially ignited the motive in me to officially resign from my position.

What changed me was when I talked to another colleague that shared almost identical opinions to me. This coworker had a similar view, yet never bothered to change.

"I gave up on all my dreams. This is the place where my last dream died." This is what she said to me. She put on a face, but I could see beyond the facade. I wanted to go back to her and ask her, "Why stay here?" I never did. I pray for her happiness and her ability to dream. I had reached a point in my life where I felt a push to help other people. I realized that we are made for more than the superficial. We are made for more than to be in this constant state of misery. Life is short and it is a gift from God, and we should make the best of this time that we are given.

When I talked with this woman, she informed me that she gave up every dream she had ever to make it to the top at this place. I asked her why she had never quit. How could someone give up? How could anyone never go for her passions? She told me she tried but failed. I rebutted with, "Why not go back and try again?" but she was fixated on the idea that her dreams were meaningless. To pursue such dreams, was stupid, according to her. She gave up on marriage. She gave up on owning a home. She gave up on having a family. My heart goes out to her. If you are reading this, please never give up. Keep pushing, keep persisting, keep moving forward.

I realized that some individuals do not want to grow. Some people don't want to change. Change is uncomfortable. Many choose to stay in situations that bring about suffering. I refuse to be part of that. This is why I began my journey to change my life. I began this journey that I am still on. The journey that I am on is to reach my potential, to lead, and to inspire others for the glory of God.

I put in my two-week notice, packed some belongings at my desk, and waved goodbye to corporate. To leave corporate was to leave security. I had it all yet I was missing something. I was venturing out on a new path away from stability. This allowed for clarity of mind. I had to get adjusted to living without the "stable lifestyle". I would have to make long-lasting changes for the sake of my mind and body, but it all led to the ultimate outcome. I became free.

My life began to go in a different direction. I'm still learning and I'm still growing. There have been changes that have happened in my mindset, my faith in God has never been stronger, and the Word of God has completely transformed me from the inside out. The knowledge carried between these pages can help you discover your purpose and reach your potential. Whatever it is you are destined to become is within you, God placed it there. If you are ready to bring about the changes in your life to achieve, I welcome you to begin your journey. Our time in this life is limited, but the opportunities are limitless.

You are made for more

1

The Problem

Life is short. People are wasting their time, they do not realize their potential, and they are squandering the gifts, abilities and opportunities that they have been given by God. They waste themselves away by focusing on materialism, other meaningless pursuits, and distractions.

This phrase has been repeated to you over and over again — it was for me. Likely you have heard this phrase hundreds of times as well. Humanity tends to think of these things but, it is rare that most of them have a firm enough grasp on it to accurately implement the true value of it in their lives. You may be one of those human beings.

Statistically speaking, we have approximately eighty years to live on Earth. You may have less time, and if you are lucky, you may undergo this human experience for much longer. How long you live here on Earth, is unknown by everyone but God. I don't mean to be negative here, I mean to be honest. Regardless, everything will come to an end. We all have an appointed time under the sun which we are to live on Earth. This is simple, yet hard to accept.

(Ecclesiastes 3:1 NIV) "There is a time for everything, and

a season for every activity under the heavens." This verse addresses appointed times; a time to be born and a time to die. Those words are truth, and they are a reminder of how precious life is. When we are placed here on Earth by God, we are given a set amount or an appointed time to live here on the Earth. Whether you are good or bad, tall or short, whatever culture you come from, we have set times for our lives. I do not say this as a discouragement. May you be encouraged! Live out your potential. God has given each of us gifts and abilities, and we should make the most of each of them.

The human experience on Earth comes with perks. We have opportunities. We can see the wonders that range from the beautiful architecture in Italy, the Moai on Easter Island, to the diverse and extravagant nightlife of New York City. We can do so much in this life! Our experience allows us to feel the crisp autumn air, to the perspiration that drips down the back of our necks on the first beach day of summer. When we witness the seasons change, we often overlook how special that concept is, "To everything there is a season".

Consider our senses. We can hear wonderful sounds. We can taste good food and drink. We can see the beauty and grandeur of the world. We can touch and smell different things. We are made to live and experience.

I highly recommend that everyone takes time to go outdoors and to look at nature. A vast amount of beauty exists here on Earth. From the Grand Canyon to the ocean blue, to the birds of the air, to the diversity of people, human beings have much to encounter. I'm always amazed at hearing about people who travel the world; they see different cultures, sites, and wonderful things in the world. Maybe you have listened to the great music, or read some of the great works throughout history. Imagine what you can learn and experience in this life. If you have never experienced any of these things, this might be a time for you to start.

As I mentioned before, we have approximately eighty years on Earth. At the time of writing this book, it is currently the year 2020, and I am approaching thirty years old. That means I have enjoyed twenty-nine winters so far. Consequently, this means, I may only be able to enjoy another fifty more or less. Pretty crazy, right?

When you break it down, if the average life expectancy is 80 years, that means that we will have 80 Summers, 80 Winters, 80 Springs, and 80 Falls. That does not sound like a lot of time.

It does not matter whether you are rich or poor, black or white, tall or short, male or female, we are all given the same amount of time a day. It makes you think about how you are spending your days, your moments, and ultimately your life.

Each time the season changes to the next, I am reminded that there is a limited amount that I have left to enjoy.

As I mentioned Ecclesiastes 3:1 earlier, I felt that it appropriate to list some of the great works of the wisdom of Solomon, found in the pages of Scripture. I am a huge fan of Solomon and his work. Some of you are familiar with these verses. If you are not, I invite you to read these eight verses from a deep and heavy book of wisdom literature, Ecclesiastes.

A Time for Everything

There is an appointed time for everything. And there is a time for every event under heaven—

A time to give birth and a time to die;

A time to plant and a time to uproot what is planted.

A time to kill and a time to heal;

A time to tear down and a time to build up.

A time to weep and a time to laugh;

A time to mourn and a time to dance.

A time to throw stones and a time to gather stones;

A time to embrace and a time to shun embracing.

A time to search and a time to give up as lost;

A time to keep and a time to throw away.

A time to tear apart and a time to sew together;

A time to be silent and a time to speak.

A time to love and a time to hate;

A time for war and a time for peace.

(Ecclesiastes 3:1-8 NASB)

The seasons are precious, and viewing them in the context of these verses has allowed me to truly understand that life is short. Life is precious as well. It certainly would appear that the seasons mentioned are parameters that are set for us living under the sun, or living here on Earth. As we live under the sun, may we find purpose in our life.

Since life is precious, we must think, speak, and act in such a way that goes beyond the superficial, the mundane, and the shallowness of life. Let us be encouraged to make the best of this life.

Another verse that comes to mind is (James 4:14 NASB) which goes on to say "Yet you do not know what your life will be like tomorrow. You are just a vapor that appears for a little while and then vanishes away." When we consider millions, billions, or the concept of Eternity, living 80 years is simply a mist. And though we are a vapor that appears and vanishes, we can still live life to the fullest. We are made for more in this life more than a finite existence on this Earth.

Our culture teaches us that we must "keep up with the Joneses". If we fail to follow what others are doing, we are seen as inferior. This is a part of the illusion that I illuminated in the introduction. If one's dreams do not adhere to society's standards, we sometimes become afraid. Since no two people are the same, how can anyone become exactly like another? I do not know who the Joneses are. Honestly, my happiness is not measured by my ability to follow people whom I do not know or care for. Even if I were very close to the Joneses, I would hope that our relationship is far deeper than the material, the education that I have, and the work that I do. What a sad and pathetic way to live life, to measure yourself by the standards and the lifestyle of another.

Through the pursuit of materialism, one can become enslaved. I once knew an entitled young woman. I had gotten to know her and I had seen how her happiness was contingent on things. She came from a wealthy family, and her parents were able to pay for a particularly extravagant lifestyle. Her mom or dad would buy her the finest clothes, the newest cars, or trips, yet she always wanted more. Sadly, nothing was ever enough for her. The moment her parents would tell her no, her entire world came crashing down. Her situation was more extreme. I realized that people can truly become enslaved by materialism, in the same way, that they can become enslaved by other desires. The pursuit of worldly pleasures, fame, fortune, and other endeavors are but a few examples of what people seek under the sun.

When I was leaving corporate, I told many co-workers that I was leaving for something better. My idea of something better was to live a more fulfilled life. I wanted to take ownership and responsibility for the life that God had given. One co-worker was upset and believed that I would be unable to have something better. This was his biased opinion. I had learned from leaving that not everyone will agree with your chosen path. I felt that my coworker had a good heart, but he knew a mere part of me.

One co-worker suggested that I see a therapist. "How could you leave all this? You have everything here!" When my co-workers said this, I was actually shocked by his response. I felt that I deserved support in making such a decision instead, I got staunch resistance. I will never forget the way that he responded- he wanted to persuade me but my mind was made up. This individual felt that the way I could do better would be to have a position that had superior benefits, superior pay, and more stability. Unfortunately, I wanted something much deeper and fundamental. This fundamental longing that I believe is in all of us.

We should never give up, and never give in. I believe that I was actually going against the grain. When you choose to go after your God-given potential and find your purpose for life, it would appear that you are going against the grain. When you go against the grain, some will support you, but many will put you down. Some will think that you are crazy. A reminder: we do not have to follow what culture deems right. We can pave our own way. Try hard to avoid the discouraging questions and the criticism that people will put your way. Instead, feel sorry for the ones who may be trying to impress their own happiness upon you. I have found in my life, some people are truly miserable. These people will do everything within their power to make sure that you are miserable as well. What a pathetic and sad way for someone to live, to make themselves feel better about themselves by putting other people down. To me, these things are nothing more than petty.

When individuals dedicate their lives to be accepted by others, they tend to drift without realizing it. I have found in my experience that when you follow the crowd, you will tend to compromise your authenticity. We do not have to live for someone else. Instead, we should do everything within our power, to find a life that is fulfilling, full of joy, happiness, and a life that is allowing for you to reach your God-given potential. For me personally, it is my desire to live a life that is God-honoring and God-glorifying in everything that I do. I am reminded of this verse from (Colossians 3:17 NASB) that says "Whatever you do in word or deed, do all in the name of the Lord Jesus, giving thanks through Him to God the Father." I live my life as close to this verse as I can. I constantly tell people that in everything that we do, we are to do in excellence for the glory of God.

Some people are unaware that fundamental parts of our society such as social media contribute to our mindless pursuits. Many people are brainwashed by the media. It teaches us to be mindless individuals and constantly bombards us with the idea that we need to "fit in". The media promotes that we need to follow the crowd without question. I wonder how many people have become slaves to the media. I'm not trying to get political in saying this, but what I am saying, is that people will take to heart what the media, advertising, and corporations are promoting. My self-worth is of more value than the ability of whether or not I can finance or lease a new vehicle. I will not find happiness in drinking vodka or smoking. It certainly is cool to buy new clothes or to follow the latest trends. When these things consume the very essence of what you are, we can get lost in the constant noise. It is nothing more than chasing the wind.

In fact, when you consider social media, we are talking about this constant stream of content. This constant flow of content is never-ending. I find that many posts are fake, artificial, and are not reality. People seem to look at an Instagram influencer, and they compare themselves. Since people are more connected than ever before, we must be mindful of technology. Does technology serve you or do you serve technology?

When I have worked with young adults and teenagers, I've seen the aftermath and the effects of being bombarded by social media statuses, influencers, and the like. It is hard to accept yourself for who and what you are when you compare yourself to the millions of likes and followers that other people have on social media. I am in no way saying that social media is bad, but we have to be careful. Social media is but a tool that we can use, and if not used correctly, it can be detrimental to people, young adults and teenagers are even more susceptible to the ills of social media. It does not stop there. Just think of young children and how they are being raised with more technology.

I think about the world my son will grow up in all the time. I think about how he will be raised with more technological advancements than I ever had. I hope and pray that my wife and I will raise him to understand that there exists more to life than social media. My wife and I desire to live a life where we control our technology, instead of letting our technology control us. This is a challenge for everyone. I pray that you are not enslaved by anything, including technology.

If you go against the culture, people will question. People will doubt and put you down when you do something different. I had doubts in my mind when I was pursuing something different. I am reminded of a quote by Thomas Edison. "Five percent of people think; ten percent of people think they think; the other eighty-five percent would rather die than think."

I pray that you are not a part of the eighty-five percent! I encourage you to be a part of the 5% of people who think. Be the best person that you can be. Use your gifts, your talents, your abilities your knowledge, your skills, and the information that you have acquired to become all that you are meant to be. I believe in God, and that we were made in the image of God. I believe that every one of us has been given a plethora of time, talents, and treasures. With all that we are given, why not use all that we have to the best of our ability? We should make a greater impact on others' lives and hope that they do the same for us.

What stands out to me from the earlier quote is eighty-five percent. It is crazy to know that such a percentage of the population exists. I am not sure if this quote is true or not, but I do believe is that some people do not think at all. These are the people who mindlessly follow what the media and what culture promotes. I mean, you can say that these are people who are sheep, and they do not ever take any time to think. Do not take part in their illusion, their fantasy, or their way. I truly pray that if this 85% rule is true, that people can become more aware, and more mindful of the importance of the beauty of life. I pray that this 85% will come to use their minds and the potentialities that come with it.

Proverbs 14:12 has always had a profound impact on my life. It goes on to say in the ESV that "There is a way that seems right to a man, but its end is the way to death." for so many people live life in such a way that seems or appears right to them. It certainly seems right that if I buy the newest model car that I will be happy. It seems right that if I get a divorce, I will be happy. It also seems right that if I get yet another degree, Masters or doctorate that I will appear happy. It also seems right that if I pursue worldly pleasures that I will be happy, but it's like many other pursuits that can end up in emptiness. Living a life chasing after the wind, is meaningless as Solomon writes in Ecclesiastes. May we become better than that. May we become mindful and understand that life is beautiful. Your life is full of purpose and potential.

A musician may stop writing and creating music because they are told that they will never make it big. An artist may be told that they may never make it big, and walk away from their creativity. Many people give up their dreams. Many people give up their ambitions, their passions, and their dreams of their potential. Some sell out and become less than they are capable of becoming. Some become fake and inauthentic. It is my hope and it is my prayer that you will never sell out. May you never settle, and may you see to it that you will seek something higher. May we seek that which is higher than the shallow, or the vanity in this world.

In our pursuit of meaningless things, we become afraid to reach our God-given potential. People long for the acceptance of others, or we are afraid to venture out and seek something higher. With social media and technology now, we are in this constant fog. For many people, there really are so many distractions from people and things.

I will be the first to admit that technology can be a huge distraction for me. I am no better than you are, and I struggle with the constant need to check on Facebook, Instagram, Twitter, and any other social media platforms. It seems like all of this technology is similar to chains. These chains are holding us down from being aware of the life that we are given. Yes, it's cool to see a video of a cat, or checking in on your family. If we are habitually glued to our phones, it can hold us back from being all that you are meant to be. We have to be careful about how much technology we use in our daily lives. I pray that technology may never enslave you, but can be a tool that can be used for good. We do not have to partake in following the way of the world. We can embark on a journey that is much different than what the world has to offer.

A verse that I love from the Word of God is (Romans 12:2 NKJV) "And do not be conformed to this world, but be transformed by the renewing of your mind, that you may prove what is that good and acceptable and perfect will of God." This verse is always encouraging to me because we should not conform to this world. Many things that this world offers that is unhealthy and meaningless. There exists another way. I have found my own spiritual walk that when I pursued the wisdom of Scripture, a relationship with God and I draw near to the Creator, that I find purpose. I have found fulfillment, happiness, and joy with God. I have seen my life completely transformed from the way that I think to the way that I speak, and the way that I am around other people. In the same manner and in the same way, I do believe that God can certainly transform your life when you seek him. We should all be encouraged to seek things that are higher than the meaningless pursuits of the world. Seek purpose. Pursue potential. Find God. Discover Life.

After years of being enslaved to the culture that has been created around us, we might lose sight of who and what we are at the core. One must first commit to taking ownership and responsibility for your life in order to excel on the path of reaching and discovering one's purpose. I once heard that responsibility is your ability to respond. I have forever taken that to heart. When life comes our way, do we respond, or do we react? Many people react to life. To respond is to think and consider before acting. May we learn the art of response and not necessarily reaction.

Think, discern, and consider your life! You must realize that you have ownership of your life! You are the captain of your own ship. You can rise to the occasion. God gave you this ability. Respond! People willingly became enslaved to the controlling culture that we live in. People willingly give up control for another person. I have seen it several times. You can break free from this mindset. Do not wallow in the fact that your actions led you to your current situation, as everything we go through happens for a reason. There many things that we simply are powerless to control. We are unable to control what is outside of us. We can control who we are. We can control what we do. We can control if and how we respond to life.

You grow from your hardships. You must accept that it is okay that you have been living a life that you expected fulfillment from but were unable to get. The past has happened. We simply are unable to change the past.

No one is able to rewrite the past. We can however learn from the past. What matters now is taking the step to realize what you can do moving forward. You can break free of old mindsets, and begin to live a life that will bring true satisfaction to you. God has given you the power to reach your highest potential. This journey will take time and effort. The journey will have its hills and valleys. There will be trials and tribulations. Will it be easy? No, but keep moving forward. It will be worth it.

The next step consists of committing time to study and learning to add to your growth and understanding. It's time to go against the grain and to seek things that are higher and nobler.

When I left my corporate job to start over I had decided I wanted to change and no longer be a slave to society any longer, and it was viewed as crazy. It goes to show you how deep this mindset goes. People around me were worried about me because they thought that something was wrong with me. Nothing was wrong with me. I wanted a peace that God promises a life that is changed forever.

This is your time to do things that go against what you are used to! Do not let the fear of doing something different stop you. You may have dreamed of doing such activities your entire life, but have never dedicated time to do so. It is time to have more action, less talk. We are all here for a purpose, and it is up to us to unlock it with the mental, emotional, physical, and spiritual capacity we are given. And let me tell you that I firmly believe that every gift comes from God. (James 1:17 NIV) "Every good and perfect gift is from above, coming down from the Father of the heavenly lights, who does not change like shifting shadows." Can you imagine how you would live your life if you could never fail? Can you imagine your life if you succeeded at all you tried?

It is time for us to begin on a path of light, truth, and life. Let us begin on a journey of becoming all that we are meant to be for the glory of God. Let us come to realize that our lives are precious, and we have got to make the best of this life while we are here on this Earth. The decisions that we make today will affect the life that we live tomorrow and for the rest of our lives. But keep in mind that it's never too late to turn your life around and choose better.

When I began my journey, I was scared, but I have to tell you that it was worth it. I am glad that I am no longer working in corporate America. Working a 9-5 job was for a season. I had to learn how not to live to know how to live life better.

God has given you many gifts, and let us be encouraged that with all that we have, all of our abilities are but tools that we should learn to master. Like a woodworker learns to master his craft, we should become confident in the business of life. We are uniquely designed beings, and all made for a purpose. It is up to you to break free of the enslavement and unlock the potential hidden within you. Life can be a wonderful journey. Make every effort to make the best of it. Live life without regrets. Go out and do. Go for it. Reach for the prize.

2

Time

Time is a wonderful gift from God. Never waste time. Be mindful of the beauty of the gift of time. Never waste your precious time.

We come from God into the human condition. I always find it to be amazing how the Word of God speaks to this. (Jeremiah 1:5 NIV) goes on to say "Before I formed you in the womb I knew you, before you were born I set you apart; I appointed you as a prophet to the nations." This passage of Scripture sticks out to me as profound. God knew us before we were born? According to this passage in Scripture, God knew us. He knows us all of us- the past, present, and future. The idea that God knows who we are and what we're capable of and gives us life, is amazing.

I believe in a God that knows us, loves us, and gives us the chance to reach our potential. God is the giver of life. God is good and in His goodness, he gives us much. Every person is different with what they are given. We have got to take responsibility for our lives. It is up to you to "Seek ye first the kingdom..." As mentioned in (Matthew 6:33 KJV) or to pursue a path "That seems right..." (Proverbs 14:12 NKJV).

Many Christians who talk theology talk about the sovereignty of God, and the Free Will of man. For me personally, I believe that there exists a balance between predestination and personal accountability. I believe that the Bible has many verses to prove both free will and predestination. I constantly tell people that God is sovereign. I tell people that God is in control and takes care of the big-picture stuff such as the creation of the universe, setting forth the heavens and the earth into motion. I also acknowledge that God desires for us to be responsible or good stewards of all that we have. To me, stewardship includes life. God does give us thinking minds, hearts to love, and choices to make. With those choices, God empowers us to make decisions. God allows us to take ownership and responsibilities for our lives. I understand that not everybody agrees with this, but these are my own personal convictions and conclusions that I have come to through the pursuits, study, and walk with God. With personal responsibility, comes accountability. We need to consider our choices and the outcome for what we put into our lives.

Ultimately, the choice is up to you. I do believe that every one of us has a choice to make. Each day, there exists thousands of choices from every moment in the course of our life. Are you going to pursue a life that is good or life that is evil? You have to ask yourself if you are going to seek God, or if you are going to seek a path of destruction as mentioned in Scripture. Many of these decisions, I am unable to make for you. I am not you. Only you can choose. Choose wisely. I have met many people who have pursued one path or another. In my personal experience, I have found that the more that I have drawn near to God and the pages of his word, the more my life has transformed.

As I've mentioned earlier, we typically are given 80 years to live on this Earth. Even though we have virtually limitless possibilities out there, one thing remains: we have a limited amount of time in this life. Time is the most beautiful resources that we have been given. Time is something that exists as a gift from God. We have been placed here on Earth for a limited amount of time. It would seem that the life that we live here on Earth is but critical, and the decisions that we make here under the sun will determine what happens in this life and the next.

It does not matter if you are rich or poor, young or old, each day, we are given the same amount of time, 24 hours. When we think of this, we must consider the amount of time that we are given in a day, and realize that it is the only resource that will end. The sun will rise and the sun will set. At the beginning of the day, is the beginning of this one day that you will only have. And at the setting of the sun, it is the conclusion of the day that God has given to you. Another day, another twenty-four hours gone. Did you live it well?

Relationships may plummet, but new relationships can be made. We can constantly chase after the money or other pursuits, but time can never be bought. Time will end. We all have an appointed set amount of time. We can live our life until it runs out. I like to think of the image of an hourglass. When our lifeglass is up, so is your time here on Earth. I encourage you that as you are living your life, thinking about what quality of life you are living, how you want to be remembered, and where you are going after this life.

It is important to understand that we can make a ton of money. In fact, we have unlimited possibilities for making money. We also have much potential for living the life that we want. As for our mortality, in the life that we are given, no one has been able to cheat death. Sure, there have been many efforts and advances in technology. We have seen our life span and life expectancy grow! This is exciting to know this. What an accomplishment for mankind. The issue though? We are still mortal. Imagine living to one-hundred, one-hundred twenty, or two-hundred years old! This too is but a drop in the ocean of eternity.

A verse that sticks out to me, and is hard for anyone to read, comes from (Ecclesiastes 6:3 NASB) says, "If a man fathers a hundred children and lives many years, however many they be, but his soul is not satisfied with good things and he does not even have a proper burial, then I say, 'Better the miscarriage than he'…" This, from the biblical account goes to show that we should all seek a life of fulfillment and purpose. A life without purpose is meaningless. A life without God is but a waste. We need both. We should live a life of fulfillment and strive to reach our potential.

In my own personal spiritual journey, I think about the idea that we are given a limited amount of time here on the earth. We should be mindful of the possibility of Heaven. We should live a life that is seeking first the kingdom of God, and we should pursue a relationship with God. It would be better to wager the possibility of getting into heaven, over wasting my life away with meaningless pursuits. Surely, the business of life should not be taken lightly. You are only given one life to live, so live it to the best of your ability. Consider that there must be something beyond this life. I personally believe in life after death. I promote the idea that we should live a fulfilled life here on earth and seek the life after this. I believe in heaven and I believe that you too should seek it.

Humans often overlook the scarcity of time. Dreams and goals are pushed to the side for the temporary enjoyment of the distractions in this world. How often do we as people, waste our time? How often do we find that we are spending our precious time on things that are useless? People tend to get distracted, derailed, or demotivated with futile things like alcohol, drugs, pornography, sex to name a few. For many, it does not have to be that extreme. Some people are lazy. Others spend too much time watching TV, social media, YouTube, and other forms of entertainment. Whatever the case may be, people shift their focus from realizing their potential and seek other things. May we be careful not to get scammed, conned, or distracted from finding meaning.

The entire idea of being consumed is a real concept for many. So many people are consumed by technology, addicted to different forms of drugs, and distractions. I encourage you to find and live a life that is full of meaning and purpose.

Consider this idea of entertainment: television, social media, magazines, and the like. We live in an age of information overload. So much information is bombarding us in our culture now. We are in the information age. Much of the content that is out is useless. Much content now is negative. I tell you that there have been many times I have gone online or watched TV and gotten depressed or angry. This negativity out there can suck the life out of you. Life is meant to be lived, experienced, and explored. I do not find any meaning in knowing the latest fads, trends, or gossip. Not only that, I feel as though media outlets want to bring you down and indoctrinate you. Life has so much more value than this.

When considering television, just think of the news networks and this constant stream that people are taking into their very lives. We find that many shows that really are about drama. Not only that, but we also have news networks that proclaim and promote negativity. What a way for my mind, and yours as well, to be constantly poisoned. Personally, I make every effort I can to make sure that I am not taking part in watching the news, or reality TV. Can you imagine the scope of how much influence the media has on people?

If you think about it, the typical American household has multiple televisions, computers, tablets, and cell phones. It would almost appear that we have more devices than we have people in a given home. I don't have statistics to back this up, but I do see this as an observation from my own personal life, and the people that I have met throughout the course of my life. With the rise of more and more technological advances in our culture, I believe that this trend will continue.

People need to take time away from their technology. As time continues, more people will not know what life is like without technology. It is important to disconnect from time to time. During the week, I make sure that I spend quality time with my wife, my son, and other members of my family.

Sometimes, I will go places where cell phone signal and internet connection is unavailable. These experiences force me to be in the present moment. I cherish these moments because they are real. Do real life. I can record and document how to ride a horse, but riding a horse in real life is always going to be different.

Technology has its benefits. It is only when technology starts to consume you that it becomes a problem. Since so much of our technology is new, the long term effects are just unknown. Cigarettes can smoke you. Technology can consume you. Drugs can abuse you. When these things become the center of your very being, a problem exists.

I do go on social media, but I do make every effort to not be on it all the time. So many times I have been on social media, scrolling, and scrolling, only to see that my screentime has consumed most of my day. Rather than suggest all social media is bad I am suggesting that we should be mindful of the time that we are spending on Twitter, Instagram, Facebook, TikTok, and whatever social media platforms we are using.

I have wasted countless hours and days on social media. Social media should be a tool, and we should be aware of how much time we spend on it. I once downloaded an application to see how many times I checked my phone, and I realized that I would look at my phone about a hundred fifty times a day. To me, that number was shocking. I could have easily spent about two and a half hours on my phone. Sadly, most of the reasons I check my phone are for unproductive ones. To be honest, I do struggle with technology, and I wonder how many people who are reading this have the same struggle. May we become empowered to use technology as a tool, rather than to be enslaved by the thing that was meant to serve us. I am very concerned about people who are young and are growing up with this constant bombardment of content. May they be empowered.

Ecclesiastes 1:9 states, "What has been will be again, what has been done will be done again; there is nothing new under the sun." I place this verse here simply because much content is meaningless. Much of the "entertainment" in the world is a distraction; a waste of time. Life has so much more meaning than this! I believe that we all should become aware of how much time we waste on meaningless things. The moment we begin to see how much time we waste, the closer we become at managing our time better.

A lot of the problems and issues that people ran into a hundred years ago, will be the same issues that people run into today. We should be aware that people throughout the centuries and throughout history have wasted their lives away. People have been wasting their time regardless of the entertainment medium. We should be mindful of the time that we waste despite the change in technology. At the end of my life, and I hope that at the end of your life, you will look back at it and can confidently say that you lived your life to the fullest. What a waste of precious time, and what a waste of a life to just throw it away at things that are meaningless, things that are unimportant, and things that are petty.

If all these technological resources are placed right in front of us, why not use it to benefit instead of using it to waste time? We are to be stewards of that which we have been given.

I am a firm believer that each one of us has been given so much. Life is but a gift, and alongside life, comes many perks, benefits, skills, abilities and the list goes on and on. Use them!

I'm reminded of how Jesus Christ mentions to his disciples the parable of the talents. Matthew 25:14-30 goes on to talk about how the three servants were given different talents. What I find to be very interesting about this, is that the concept of talent was a form of money during Biblical times. Nowadays, we look at talents as skills and abilities, and I find that if we observe this parable of the talents, we can still apply this to the modern-day context. This concept is very simple, that we are given much, and we are to use what we are given to the best of our ability. I tend to think that even if we fail, we continue to do the best that we can. Nobody is perfect. We will feel a sense of achievement and accomplishment by giving everything we do our all. Let us give life everything. Let us never quit. Never give up. Let God be glorified by you doing your personal best at everything in life.

We are to make the best of our life, and the time that we have been allotted. I advise, I encourage and I plead that you make the best of your time. I encourage that if you do not know what your gifts, talents, and abilities are, that you can see to it that you will search within. Go ahead and explore, and discover who you are, and what you are capable of. I believe that we even have it in ourselves so much potential that is untapped. Thomas Edison can be quoted as saying, "If we did all the things we are capable of, we would literally astound ourselves." What an amazing idea. Can you just imagine astounding yourself by reaching your God-given potential?

As noted by the problem in the previous chapter we are afraid. We are sometimes afraid to use the time we have been given because we feel we will fail or let others down. We may have a gift, or we may have an ability, and often we become afraid of an undesired outcome. When we venture out into the world, we will fall, we will falter, or we will fail. What matters is what we do after that undesired outcome.

We spend about a third of our lives sleeping. That is a third of your life that you are unconscious. If a third of your life is used for sleeping, how will you use the remaining two-thirds? You are awake and you are aware, but will you act? When you think about it, we are given 24 hours a day, but eight hours of it is given towards sleeping. For many of us, 8 hours are dedicated to working a nine-to-five job, or a specific set amount of hours that we dedicate to the work that we do. Even in working a nine-to-five job, we still have eight hours that we can explore, learn, or really do whatever we want to. Let us not waste any of the time that we are given. I am motivated by the fact that I have 16 hours that I have full control over. I don't know about you, but I do enjoy having a good night's sleep.

Let's break down the typical path that most people follow throughout their lifetime. We have approximately eighty years on Earth eighty new years, eighty summers, eighty winters. Most people graduate from high school when they are eighteen years old. From there, you will attend university for approximately four years and will be hoping to grasp onto that high paying job at twenty-two. Now, if you're lucky, you will get to retire at sixty-seven years old. That leaves you with a remaining thirteen years. By this time, you may be a part of the statistics of declining health in humans, and will not have the energy to pursue the dreams you put off for your whole life. Was it worth it all chasing the wind? Was it worth neglecting the things that money can't buy, for things money can buy? Was it worth working in a job you hated? Was it worth never trying something new, never knowing the answer? You do not want to look back at your life wondering, "What if I ___ ", as so many people do. Our lives are short. We spend each day putting off the desires of our soul and focus on being wealthy even if it brings about misery. Instead, let us use the tools we humans were given by God, and realize the potential you were given. Make something out of it, whatever it may be. Whatever it is that you know you are meant for at your core. Make the best of your life!

I want to note here, that some people are perfectly happy by following this framework, or this model of living. If this is something that you desire to do, and you find fulfillment in happiness in the choices that you make, I commend you for that. If you are finding that you are not happy, fulfilled, and you feel as though something is missing in your life, then I encourage you to seek after such a life. Seek God and the things that will bring you fulfillment and joy in this life. I do believe that every person has a different motivation and a different calling. We are all called to do different things. Some are called to the typical 9 to 5 jobs. Others are not. This is a decision that only you can determine.

Albert Einstein noted, "Everybody is a genius. But if you judge a fish by its ability to climb a tree it will live its whole life believing that it is stupid." I bring up this quote as a reminder that we are all called to live a certain life. I believe the framework that our culture promotes can be beneficial to some but not good for all. Different types of intelligence and different skills exist for such a diversity of people. This is one of the beautiful facts of life.

Along with the pages of Scripture, I enjoy reading different books on different topics. Something that I found that I wanted to mention is the Law of Affection. This is very different from the Law of Attraction. In his book, *The Millionaire Fastlane*, MJ DeMarco introduces this simple, yet profound concept that is the Law of Affection. Simply put, the more people you affect, the better chance of becoming successful you will become. Earl Nightingale also wrote that "Our rewards in life will be in exact proportion to our service." Instead of trading time for money, render the best service you possibly can. Once we get out of this time-money concept, our lives will then change. Let us consider how we can be the greatest influence on people. Our lives can have a tremendous impact on people whether we know it or not. We therefore should have the heart to serve other people to serve people. The Scriptures call us to Love God and Love, People. In the same manner, we should serve God and serve others.

With such ideas and concepts from people let us inspire those in our lives. We all should discover what our purpose is. God gives us a purpose in life. He has a plan for each of us. We all can influence other people positively. We can help others. When we live a life full of purpose, living out your potential, you can make a tremendous difference in people's lives. Imagine using your God-given potential for good. Always consider how you can leave a lasting impression on others through your own actions. Let us live lives that impact others.

When following this, it is important to always make the best use of your time. Time should never be taken for granted, as you are guaranteed to never get it back. Time is a gift, and time is precious. Do not let the negatives of this world steal your precious time away from you. In my experience, I have found that when I take time focusing on the positive, I do not think so much of the negative.

God has granted us all with time, but not all of us have been given the same amount. From God, we are placed on Earth, to experience life here under the sun. Each one of us has been sent here to experience this very lifetime. We even have the chance to seek God and to seek first the kingdom of God as Scripture mentions. God continues to mold us and form us into the person we are meant to be.

Some of us live long lives, and some babies leave this Earth just a few short months after they are born. God has planted us here for a certain amount of time here. Let us value what time we have here. You never know what tomorrow holds, so enjoy today. Enjoy time with your friends and family and make life the best you can.

We don't know when our expiration date is. Let us live this life seeking and living out that potentiality placed in us from God. I pray that we all grow and come closer to reach your God-given potential. Personally, I spend a lot of my time reading, praying, studying, and improving my life. Helping myself grow and improve, I am taking control of my life. I am taking ownership of what God has granted to me. I am responding with ability. I do this to have a greater impact on others.

I enjoy being around those who are moving forward. I enjoy seeing people learn and grow. It is great to pursue knowledge, wisdom, and understanding. I do this to make my life better, but also help people with the life that they live. I will continue to promote the idea that we should take ownership and responsibility of the life that God has given. This goes along with the idea of being a steward. As a steward, it is my responsibility to take care of my own life. This is because this appointed time, and this life, are but a gift. Every gift is to be appreciated. Every gift is to not be taken for granted. A gift, like any, should be received well by the gifted. We are all gifted with life. Since God gives us this life, he also gives us an ability to receive the gift of salvation.

We are put on this earth to live for a certain amount of days. We are meant to live, to learn, and to experience the human condition for a certain amount of time. We are given many gifts, so let's use them! This life that we have, we must be grateful for, but we must also make the most of the time that we are allotted. Be encouraged to live a fulfilled life with purpose and your potential. Also, consider that with God in your life, you will live a life of joy, happiness, and fulfillment in this life and the next.

3 |

Life

Life is the greatest gift that we have received from God. Live your life wisely. People can easily waste their life if they are not careful.

I remember when I was in Middle School, I knew a man highly involved in the school leadership. This man would always tell incoming and outgoing middle-schoolers to be a leader and not a follower. I remember those words to this day. We have the opportunity, and this ability to have such a profound impact on the lives around us. We should live our lives to the fullest capacity, and inspire people. We should empower people. We should encourage people to be the best that they can be. You would be amazed at how your life can have an impact on someone else.

It is easy for humans to forget that the life we are given is precious. We live in an imperfect, broken world. We are surrounded by some who were brought into this world with disabilities or mental disorders. Despite such disorders or disabilities they too can see the beauty of God's creation in their life. Some individuals may have dealt with the misery of being born into a broken family. Maybe you never had to deal with any of these hardships, or maybe you are one of these individuals. No matter where you are at in life, what situation you are going through, or what cards you have been given in this life, life is beautiful. Life is precious. Life is a gift. We can all choose to enjoy life regardless of our circumstances or situation.

It's easy to make excuses, it is easy to feel sorry for yourself. Culture teaches us that we should feel sorry for ourselves. Culture also teaches that we should remain and not improve. We are made to grow. We live, we grow, and we learn. God created us with unconditional love. I am not God, and I do not know why some people are born with imperfections, and why some people struggle more than others. I do believe that he has a reason, lessons, and every person is going to be on a different path. No two people are the same. We are all humans, but we are all different. We all are uniquely made for a purpose, to become all we can be. We are also made to seek life from God.

No matter who or what you are, where you come from or what you have been through, you still have great potential within you. God has embedded such potential and it is up to you to find it. Find it, grow it, share it. Helen Keller is a perfect example of this. A woman who endured immense battles in her life, being blind and deaf, yet she spoke. She still found the strength to reach her God-given potential. Her story is but one of many examples of people who have been able to persevere and overcome adversity. We certainly can go on and on about the numerous amount of people who have risen to greatness despite their circumstances.

We will face many battles. There will be many hills and valleys that we experience, and it is up to us to decide what we are going to do in those times. As a Christian, I am a firm believer that God is always going to be there with us in times of good and in times of bad. The Scripture mentions in Deuteronomy 31:6 "Be strong and courageous. Do not be afraid or terrified because of them, for the Lord your God goes with you; he will never leave you nor forsake you." And it is in those times when we are weak and vulnerable that we need someone who can help us. I believe in a God who will always be there. With this in mind there too are people such as friends and family who can be there as well. It is perfectly fine to get as many people as possible to help you get through any trial or tribulation in life.

Do not fall into the idea that if you are in the midst of misfortune, you will remain there. That choice is up to you. You can remain. You can rise above. You can rise to your potential. Fear not! Put aside your fears and devote time to getting out of a rut. And I encourage you to be empowered by God to be strong and to keep moving forward. May we respond by taking ownership and going through life never stopping and never turning back.

I once knew of a pastor who told me in the midst of a church split that I should never look back, but rather keep moving forward. Although the situation was terrible and not ideal, I remember those words of wisdom. I was very discouraged during this time. I found a profound strength when he advised that I never look back and to keep moving forward. I am forever grateful.

Always remain grateful. Be grateful for your life. Find ways to appreciate matters in your life. No matter how big or small, we can always find things to be thankful. My wife is a great example. She reminds me of her own life what she appreciates. She looks at a flower and sees beauty. We will go hike in the mountains, and she will listen to the birds. She always finds things to appreciate. We all should do this.

This world is imperfect. Be aware and be reminded that this world is, full of crime, war, disease, and hate. No matter what is going on in the world, the community, this country, or even in your own life, you can be empowered to respond. It took me a very long time to realize that what happens on the outside is out of my control. All I can do is take control of my own life and fully rely on God in such delicate times. Part of relying on God is to understand that many things are out of your control. This also is part of maturity. I believe that responsibility is a part of maturity. In a world where people remain ignorant, may we desire to become wise!

We should all be encouraged to be grateful for everything that we have. Just think about the simple fact that you are alive. You are here, in the present moment, and you are reading this passage. That is amazing. The fact that we are alive, is nothing short of beautiful. Sometimes I think about the fact that I am alive, and that I am here in this place at this moment doing what I am doing. We should all take time to take it all in. We are in the here and now!

You are created for a purpose. You are here for a reason. Your life is meant for more than to be held back. We do not have to put up with people trying to put us down, or holding us back from reaching our potential. Life is meant for more than this. No two people are the same. No matter what our culture teaches, or what it promotes, you are different than I am. I am different from you. This is just a basic reality that we all should understand.

So many people are alone in the world. Some people drift from place to place, with no direction in their life. I whole-heartedly believe that we should all search for meaning and purpose in our life. I have met a number of people who have no reason to live, no purpose and no direction. I have also met people who deny that life has any meaning. More often than not, these people are some of the most aggressive, angry, depressed, and lost people I have ever met. I am not writing this to be critical but as an observation. Through the pursuit of God, purpose and strive to become all that you are meant to be, there exists peace, joy, and fulfillment. I would prefer to have these emotions and motivations, rather than bringing people down. I desire to bring people up and motivate rather than to destroy. In the same manner, you have that decision to make. Will you build or will you destroy? Will you seek light or darkness? Will you seek life or will you seek death? Consider such matters.

The fact that we are alive is beautiful, and we are here for a reason. Sadly, some people refuse to believe this. I pray that you believe. I encourage you to look at it from the angle that you are here, and you are alive, and you should make the best of this life. Let us seek things that are higher, let us seek God in his wisdom, and let us live out our lives reaching our potential. Let us find a life that is but fulfilling, full of meaning, and living a life that brings us joy. I believe that we can all find that, if only we could take the time to search it out.

Many of us find ourselves in the habit of comparing ourselves. We sometimes wish we were taller. Other times we wish we had their money, their house, an attractive spouse, and the like. The list goes on and on when people seek to be the same as another. This is a terrible habit to get it, to wish you were someone else. Since God empowers you, you can pave the way to live the life that you have always wanted. You have to take charge and go out and do!

I used to struggle with obsessively comparing myself to others. I have to make sure not to get into that habit. I would look at someone's success and think that I was treated unfairly. I would tell people how I wish I had more money, a better car, and more things. Things do not bring happiness. To seek things is to seek materialism. The material world is fleeting and will fade away. Even human beings, we are not here permanently. Why should I seek things that will fade away? It took me a very long time to realize that my happiness should not be in the things that will fade away over time. The cycle will go on and on, and I will be chasing something that will never feel my need to be fulfilled. Fulfillment comes from that which is everlasting. My fulfillment comes from my walk with God.

No one is exactly the same. We are all on our own Journey. Every one of us has been placed in different circumstances and different situations. My journey, the lessons, and the path that God has set before me may be different than the person next to me, my friends, and even my family. This is just one of those realities of life. Some people that I've met have all the money in the world, yet they have a completely different battle than one that another friend of mine would have. With the situations and scenarios that we have been placed in, it is up to us to find that path of fulfillment and happiness. Let us come to a better understanding of knowing who God is and drawing near to him. God, being the giver of life, supplies you with your potential and will help you on your path of purpose.

God made you in his image. This we must accept. Learn to love yourself just as he does. This is one of the hard truths of life. I have found that I am much harder on myself than other people are, and how God is even. Because God loves me, and he forgives me when I repent the slate is wiped clean. This is absolutely remarkable. Be invigorated to live a life full of forgiveness. We should never hold grudges. We must learn from past hurt and forgive. This is a wonderful pursuit, but it is at times harder to do in practicality than it is on paper. I am human. I have my limitations. Because of these things, it can be hard for me to forgive. We are called to forgive those who have wronged us. The fact that God forgives me more than I forgive myself, is no different than how God loves me more than I love myself. We are called to love God and to love other people. Part of this love is to love yourself. Think about that. God made you as you are, and he gives you such great potential inside of you. It is up to you to decide what you are going to do with that potentiality, and what you are going to do with your life. We are called to love who we are, not in some vain conceited manner, but to have this understanding that we are who we are. Life is but a gift from God. We should never compare ourselves to other people, and we should understand that everybody has a different scenario and a different path than they are to pursue. They, just like you are to find their purpose, reach their potential, and come to God during their life.

You can use what God gave you to become the highest version of yourself. I encourage you, you who are reading this, that you've become the best version of yourself. Reach that God-given potential, because God has created you, and God is empowering you. What better way to live your life than to live it for the fullest? You were created by God, as we all are. Realize how powerful and remarkable that is.

With the limited amount of time that we are given here on the Earth, we are never promised tomorrow, so we must live life as though it were our last. We certainly need to see to it that we are going to give life our all, every day. We have got to live in the moment and live the best life never giving up. If you have a vision, a dream, or a goal in which you have ever wanted to live, or something that you have wanted to do, go out and do it. In fact, the Scripture calls us not to worry about tomorrow. (Matthew 6:34 CSB) "Therefore don't worry about tomorrow, because tomorrow will worry about itself. Each day has enough trouble of its own." I always find this verse from Scripture to be very inspiring. I'm only going to be young once, and so I'm going to make the best of my youth. I'm going to make the best of every season that I'm in, and at least do the best I can. This does not mean that I'm going to fail, I will falter and I will fail, and I probably will do it many times. With that thought, we plan, we make goals, and we do everything that we can to make our dreams a reality. In that though, we are not promised tomorrow, and we live our lives as though it were our last day here on Earth.

I have always had this image in my head, like a video played in my mind. I have had this idea of being on my deathbed, and before the moment of my death, knowing that I lived my life to the best of my ability. I do not want to look back at my life thinking of what "could have been". I do not want to just exist in this constant state of fog and confusion by holding myself back. So often, people hold themselves back from what they are capable of. May you never become a person like this. Go out and shoot for the moon. Aim high. Never give up. Pursue being the best you can be in this life.

When we consider the quote that I mentioned earlier in this writing, 85% of people do not think. If this the statistic or even slightly true, that is very eye-opening. Imagine living your entire life never thinking a thought, never dreaming, never having goals or aspirations, and just going through the motions of life. This is but a sad existence. It is a reality for many. Many people live life this way. A great number of people who live their life in a constant state of fog. Sadly, a lot of people never take time to think, consider their life, or even two looks at the results of the decisions that they have made. Several people do not even understand why they are where they are in life. If we are but mindful of the consequences of our decisions, we can look back, evaluate, and come to make better decisions. To combat this ignorance of life, we must see to it that we are to help empower people to realize how precious life is. What a tragedy would it be to die never reaching your full potential. Be empowered. Empower.

Do not wonder what could have been. For some people, asking that one girl out could have been something that they should have done, do it! For others, it could have been making an effort to start your own business. Maybe, it could have been this inner desire to spend more time with family, go for it. To be empowered is to realize that you are in control of your life. God has given you this gift, and you are taking ownership of this gift.

I tend to think of my son, and how he is a little child. I get to raise him. I get the privilege to teach him. I will teach him everything I know, and I will give him opportunities to become the man he is meant to be. Even with all my efforts, the choice is up to him. I hope and pray that he will make good decisions that honor and glorify God. I will make every effort within my power to encourage him, empower him, and stay on the straight and narrow path.

I see God in a similar light. I believe that God is always there for you, and he's always wanting what is best for you. God is allowing you to make decisions. So, think and consider your choices before making any decision. To have the freedom to choose is empowering. This helps explain why evil is in the world. Some people choose to do evil. As for you, choose to do good. Why people choose evil? I am not sure. I am not them. What I do know is this; with every external event that happens in our life, we are to respond.

The fear of failure and the fear of rejection is something that plagues the minds of so many people. Let us remember that it is better to have tried and failed at your dream then never to have done anything at all. Some people do not even try. Part of the path to success is to try, fail, learn, make adjustments, and try again. This is similar to that famous quote that we keep trying even if we don't succeed. And I pray that for you to choose to go on this path of happiness and fulfillment, that you will never give up. To fail is but a part of success, and we always keep moving forward to the prize.

We all have free will, we all have to make decisions in our lives. How you choose, is up to you. Choose wisely. Consider what is wise. Do the best you can. Seek counsel if need be. Remember, to not choose is to make a choice. I say this to encourage you. Be a person who starts. Be a person who tries. Be one who never gives up.

Life can be hard. You will run into obstacles. You will have challenges. There will be hills and valleys in life. This is reality. Keep moving forward. Seek life. Go for your potential. Seek God. Do it.

4

Abilities and Talents

God is the giver of life. God is light. God is good. God also gives you abilities and talents. Such talents vary from person to person. How you are gifted is unique to you. How I am gifted is unique to me. There really exists such a diversity of these gifts and abilities. We should all be motivated to use these gifts. Learn, grow, and show. You may be able to create magnificent pieces of art, sing out melodies, touch others with words, make people laugh and so much more. I'm certainly amazed by the number of singers, musicians, artists, writers, and other creative individuals out there. There certainly exists an abundance of talented people. Never neglect your abilities and talents.

Some people feel useless because they do not have a certain skill. We are all given a certain level of talent. We are all able to work hard and nurture specific abilities. We also can learn, develop, and grow new skills. It really depends on the situation. Certainly, within each one of us, we possess talents. Have you taken inventory of the skills, abilities, and talents you have? If only we but take the time to discover these things. People need to discover what they can do.

To master a specific talent, spend time developing it. Put in the work - research, study, practice. It is never a waste of time to enrich yourself with the abilities God has given to us. Imagine being given a car, surely you would drive it? I am sure that you would want to learn how to take care of it if it meant that much to you? What a waste for some people to be given such gifts, and never use them. Let us be people who are given gifts, use them! We certainly have got to become empowered and encouraged to take care of all that we have been given.

Pursue what it is that you would like to do. Share your passion and go for your potential. God has made you for a purpose, and it is up to you to find out what that purpose is. From finding our mission in life to discovering God and our untapped talents, we can discover much. Just imagine what you can gain when you pursue these things.

Let us never neglect our talents. For if we let these talents go to waste, we are throwing away a piece of our potentiality. If I have been given a talent, shouldn't I use it? What does it look like to use the gifts, talents, and abilities?

A song that I remember hearing when I was younger, and within it is a lyric that sticks out to me to this day. It's called, "The Sounds of Silence". Maybe you have heard it before. I think about the lyrics "People writing songs that voices never share". I would listen to that lyric and wonder to myself, "Why would anyone write a song and never share it with others?" If you do not use your talents, what a waste of life! These are some of the few things that make us unique. Live out what makes you uniquely you!

I see it all the time. I have met many people who have

tremendous talent and do not use it at all. Sometimes people are simply humble, and some people do not share because of pride. These are not the only reasons. There exist other reasons for someone not sharing their work. I was one of those people. I would write songs and never showcase it to others. I did this because I felt that my work would be rejected. I had this mindset that nothing was ever good enough. I feared rejection and that fear held me back. I write these things to encourage you to never hide your abilities.

I believe that fear holds so many people back. The fear of placing yourself out there with your work is very real. People fear rejection and criticism. Other people do not know where to start. This varies from person to person. Let us not be afraid. Let us venture out boldly in this life.

If you use what God granted you with positive means, you will find fulfillment. God loves you and when you give your work your best, God will be satisfied. We do not need to live for the approval of others. We can live life just doing the things that we love. How will you know the outcome when you do not even input? How will you reap if you do not sow?

Do not die with so much still within you. Do not leave this life wondering what if. Do not go out asking what you could have been. Simply go out and just try. Success does not come immediately but in different forms; sometimes immediate, sometimes overtime. Just going out and doing is a start. Live your life to the fullest. Give life your best. We only have one life, and we should not waste ourselves away. Life is but a precious gift, and we have a limited amount of time here on the Earth. Let us be mindful of the decisions we make with what we have been given.

Use what sets you apart from others and share it with the world. Use it to inspire others. They may be influenced to do the same - remember the Law of Affection.

"Don't die with your music still in you" - Dr. Wayne Dyer

5

The Two Verses

Two quotes I want to share with you in this chapter. These two verses are from the Word of God. They are but pieces of wisdom. I would like to take this moment to share these two verses with you. May they help you on your spiritual journey in the same way that they've helped me.

"As you think, so shall you be."

It is important to consider what you spend most of your time thinking of. What is it that occupies your mind? What is it that you choose to fill it with? Are you choosing to fill it with love or do you bombard it with negativity? Do not undermine the power of words and their effect on you.

When you constantly choose to fill your head with negative thoughts, your subconscious will latch on to that. If you choose to tell yourself that you are an idiot, worthless, untalented your mind will never forget it. Our minds are precious. We have got to be careful with what we put into our minds.

This is actually what Earl Nightingale called The Strangest Secret that "We become what we think about." Now, there have been many other writers over the course of history who have reiterated this same thought. We have got to be mindful of the things that we think about, the things that we spend our time on. Have you ever taken the time to really look at what you are thinking about? Have you ever thought about what you watch, read, or put into your mind?

When I hear quotes like this, I am reminded of how powerful our minds are. Our minds are tools that can be used for good or bad. The choice is up to us what we do with our minds. The things that people put via sound, audio, or experience, people tend to think about. When we think about it, it is only a matter of time that we become what we think.

If I tell myself something enough times, I may eventually believe it. Words can have an enormous effect. This is why we need to be mindful of what people say to us, and what we say to ourselves. The saying goes: change your thoughts, change your life. This idea is a close cousin to sowing and reaping, which I will mention a little bit later in this chapter.

From the Bible, a famous verse in the King James Version stands out to me very much. It goes like this, "For as he thinketh in his heart, so is he" (Proverbs 23:7 KJV). This goes along with the idea that we will essentially become what we think about. This is but a spiritual truth that we must understand. Through the understanding of these truths, we can make better decisions in our lives. Not only this, but we can also make help others become aware of what they think about.

Another passage in Scripture that goes along with this nugget of truth. "Do not conform to the pattern of this world, but be transformed by the renewing of your mind"

(Romans 12:2 NIV). On my own spiritual walk, there came a time where I drew closer to God, and my faith in Jesus Christ had become stronger. I have found that when I have God at the center of my life, I enter into this path of life. I have found that when God is at the center of my life, my life is fulfilled with meaning and purpose.

The more I pursue God the more God transforms me. I identify as a Christian, one who seeks Jesus Christ. I have a relationship with Christ and my desire to seek the deeper things of God. Truth is found in the Word of God.

A verse in Scripture that motivates me every time I read it or share it with another. This comes from (Proverbs 25:2 NASB) "It is the glory of God to conceal a matter, but the glory of kings is to search out a matter." This verse is but encouraging to me personally. I hope that this verse, you will find encouraging as well. This verse means that God will hide things. God will conceal things in the pages of his word and throughout his creation. In the concealment of these things, it is as though God has hidden these matters for people do discover. I not only think of the deeper things that have been discovered through the wisdom of the Word of God but the discoveries that have been made throughout history. Much more is to be discovered in our existence. Not only are things hidden outside of us, but there too are things that are to be discovered within us. We are but to seek out our potential and to discover what we are capable of. Not only this but by the transformation through God, other discoveries can be made. God can transform you. God can mold you into someone greater, through his plans. Consider such things.

My life has been transformed so much when I entered into a relationship with Jesus Christ. Not only this but the more I sought after him, the more he began to mold me and change me. I am where I am today because of God guiding me. It is my prayer that God will lead and guide you. Seek him. He is there. Turn to him. He will deliver. I thank God for the transformation that has taken place in my life. With all of this being said, I am not done. I know God is continuing to mold me and to transform me from the inside out. For those of you who do not have a relationship with Jesus Christ, I encourage you to consider it. Your life will never be the same, I can assure you of that.

I have found so much meaning, happiness, and fulfillment from the Word of God. As I am writing this, I have been working through wisdom literature, and I have been so challenged by the wisdom of Solomon and the other wisdom literature books. I desire to be close to God. He loved me first. Because of this love, I strive to love him and to love other people. I hope that as you've been reading this book, you have been encouraged to reach your God-given potential, but, furthermore, to enter into a relationship with him. Be on that journey. Learn. Grow. Become.

I also want to add that going on a spiritual journey, it's a two-way street. See to it that you take ownership of your life. Take responsibility for your life. Also, seek God to help you along the way. This is why I mentioned so much about being empowered by God. You can certainly allow for God to work in you, but you also must go out and do. I firmly believe that

God will take care of the big things, and we have to take care of ourselves.

An effective way to begin the transformation of your life is by changing the way you think. You are not doing yourself any favor by speaking negatively about yourself. You also need to be mindful of people in your life that may be bringing you down. Understand that words may not seem to be a big deal. Words can have an impact. Be with people who will help and support you along the way. Stay away from people who will stop at nothing to bring you down. You are worth more than to be constantly belittled.

I once worked with a coworker who would criticize me. She would always have something negative to say about my work. I would work hard, but it would never seem to be enough. Other coworkers would ask if I was okay because some of the words that were spoken were harsh. I would always say that I was okay. I would do everything to brush it off. Over time, I did begin to doubt myself. "What if she was right and I was wrong? I mean, she did work longer than I." I reached out to my boss and ask about how I am doing in my job. He would reply that I am doing well and that I was a good worker. The unkind words continued. I eventually brought this up with my boss, and he took care of it. I still remember the words that were said to me. It was a hard situation and one that I never have forgotten. Not to worry, I no longer work at that place. Let bygones be bygones. This story is but an experience that I had. I was able to ignore the words at first, but over time, they did affect me. Eventually, the situation became unfavorable and I had to remove myself from that place of employment. In such situations, we have got to be careful of the people we spend our time with. You will be surprised how much people have an influence on yourself.

It has been said that if you tell someone something enough times, eventually they will believe it. It is only a matter of time before the words affect you. Think of the world that we live in. So much negativity in this world, especially the media. I firmly believe that the media tries to influence us. We can be influenced by the things that we watch or view on our devices.

We've got to be careful of what we put into our minds, and what we dwell upon. May we see things that are higher, things that are positive, and things that are life-giving. I really pray that you may consider what you are thinking about, and what you are putting into your mind. Certain things in this world are unfruitful, unfulfilling, and ungodly. Do you honestly want to take the risk of putting in such things that could harm yourself and even harm others? I am not going to tell you what to do, but I am at least encourage you to think about such matters. Be a part of the 5% who thinks.

Sure, we will have our bad days, bad situations, and even bad seasons. I am not encouraging you to neglect your emotions. I am encouraging you to make the best out of every situation. In certain times in my life, I've had to let go and let God. What this means, is that I've had to lay my burdens to God, the higher power.

No matter who you are, good and bad situations will happen in life. That is part of us living here in the human condition on Earth. Humans are imperfect, and quite honestly the world that we live in is imperfect. Perfection only exists in God.

Let us just keep in mind who we want to become. Let us focus and fixate our minds on becoming the best that we can be. God calls us to reach our potential and will help us out along the way. Do not underestimate the power of visualization or the power of thought or the power of imagination. Do you think of the life that you want? Do you think of your goals and dreams? I am sure you do. Do you ever sit back and think of the steps it will take to actually get there?

It is important to take time and consider how it is that you will achieve these dreams. It all begins with how you think. As a part of my journey, I desired to get into better shape and become the outgoing person I have always wanted to become. It all began with the belief that I would become that and I deserved to as well. I wrote down how I would get to that point, put forth the steps to get there and I acted as if I had already achieved it until I actually did! I went out and did the work. I did the best that I could, and I did struggle at times. In fact, I still struggle with my weight to this day, but I do the best that I can.

"As you sow, so shall you reap"

Once you have mastered the transformation of your mind, it is time to focus on the transformation of your actions. Remember, God can and will transform your life. You too must take responsibility for your life by choosing right and living. Be a leader. Be a giver. Be an inspiration. I always like to remind myself that it is better to give than to receive. This is what Christ said in (Acts 20:35 NIV) "It is more blessed to give than receive". This is part of the idea and the concept of sowing and reaping.

When you choose to focus and work on certain aspects of your life such as marriage, friendships, business, and health, you are planting seeds into these areas. When you pour your time and attention into these areas, you are helping them grow. Think about a plant. You plant the seed into the ground. You care for it. You water it. You give the plant an appropriate amount of sun. If you are sowing into the areas of your life that you wish to grow and become fruitful, you will eventually reap from the energy you invested in it. Ask yourself, what are you sowing into?

This is one of the great truths of Life. This concept of sowing and reaping is something that we find to be applicable to most if not all areas of life. We have to be mindful, and we have to be careful about the things that we see in our lives. Are we sowing negativity into the relationships that we have currently? Are we sowing the seeds of studying for good grades at school?

Not only this, let us consider what we are reaping. What are you getting in life? Are you happy with the outcome of the things that you are doing? We certainly should consider the results of our actions. If we are not getting the results that we want, we simply have got to change what we are putting in. Want to reap differently? Sow differently.

These are but many examples and this piece of wisdom is so simple. This is what I love about wisdom. Wisdom is simple. Wisdom is transcendent of the ages. Wisdom works. The concept of sowing and reaping is a reality for this life. It is so powerful too. I believe that an entire book or collaboration of books can be written just on this concept. Not only do I believe that we will reap what we sow in this life, but we will even reap what we sow in the next life. We just have got to be careful at the things that we say, the things that we do, and who we are as a person. May we all be on a path of spiritual growth. I pray that we all will become the man or the woman that God intends for us to be. I also hope that we will think before acting. I pray that we will consider what we are sowing, and understand the consequence at what we will reap at the given appropriate time.

The concept of sowing and reaping has been known in many different forms. Some people call it input and output. Some people incorrectly call it karma. Some people even call it a consequence of our actions. No matter what you call it, it is a transcendent principle that applies to everyone. Let us learn and implement this concept. Just this piece of wisdom will change your life. Be empowered.

If you are getting an undesired outcome, look at what you can change to move forward. We always can move forward in our life. Let us move forward positively. Take a look at your actions. Are you taking responsibility for why it's not going the way you want? What are you sowing? Your actions have a direct cause for the outcomes in your life. The results of your life come from what you choose to invest your efforts and your energy into.

If one of your goals is to look and feel healthy and fit, your actions must go with that goal. If you choose to eat junk and sit on the couch all day, you are sowing an unhealthy lifestyle. This is but one of many examples out there of this concept.

If you are unable to figure out if you are sowing a desirable life, look at what you have reaped. This can be recent events or past events. View your life honestly. Are you content and proud of where you are and how you feel? If not, look at the aspects of your life which you wish to change, and begin to put your time and energy towards bettering it. It may take time, but your efforts will pay off. To bring about change in your life, you must focus on what it is that you are sowing. This simple process requires us to look back at the past and learn from it. This is an ongoing process. Consider the where, how, when, and why we do what we do. Consider the output and input.

God has given us the privilege to craft our lives and it is up to us to make it that. We get to make the decisions on what we sow in our lives. Choose wisely. We must examine these matters. We do this to become more aware. We do this to make better decisions. Surely, our efforts will not be perfect. From every outcome, can come a lesson. Every lesson can come to an adjustment. With every adjustment, is one step closer to living life better. We always can improve. We always can become better. This is part of reaching your God-given potential.

I do want to mention that we have to account for certain times where God can intervene. In the pages of Scripture, God has intervened. Sometimes, a supernatural event happens. God has intervened before. God can intervene now. God can intervene now or in the future. Sometimes things happen that are hard to explain. Divine intervention must not be ruled out as a possibility. We must consider the possibility of divine intervention.

The life that you live right now is the result of what you have done in the past. You are the way that you are because of what you put in. The actions that you have taken and the thoughts you have concentrated have all led you here. It is up to you to change your life. It is up to you to plant the seeds and take care of them. A farmers crop will grow from the scattering and nurturing of the seeds. You must nurture your thoughts and actions. Be mindful of what you sow in your life. Be mindful of your thoughts.

I truly do think and consider where I am at today. As I am writing this book, I am in the middle of the year in 2020. I began my journey back in 2017, and I still believe that things that are happening because of what I had initially sown. Sometimes we sow seeds and they take days to reap. Other times we sow the seed and it takes years to reap. It varies.

I am continuing to sow. I am doing this through continued education. I am doing this by learning, growing, and developing. I plan on not stopping. Never stop growing. Never stop learning. Continue to be on a path of becoming. We can find many ways that we can grow and improve. These decisions are up to you. Sow the Word of God. Sow knowledge. So wisdom. Sow information that can help you get from your present state to your desired state. Sow good words and actions to other people. Empower people. Encourage people to be the best that they can be. In everything that you do, be the best that you can be. You will reap what you sow. Consider other people, and consider the profound impact you have on others. Life is short. You will never really know the effect that you will have on another person.

6

Committing to Growth

To bring about continuous change into your life, you must commit to growth. This may sound easy, but it merely requires discipline. As humans, we are easily distracted and can become procrastinators. It takes great strength to push past obstacles. If you are devoted to living out your potential, your efforts will be worth it. Keep your mind fixed on the prize. Keep going and remain constant. By committing yo growth, you are bringing meaning to your life. This helps solve the problem of people wasting themself away.

It is very easy for people to become distracted with their day-to-day activities. People can get distracted by so many things. From television to social media, distractions are but common. We need to be careful. You'd be surprised how much time can be lost.

It is said that people have lower attention spans. Maybe you have heard this too. People seem to not know how to pay attention. Maybe some have forgotten or gotten used to it. From my own experience, I have found that many people are conditioned to be distracted. The art of discipline, persistence, and patience are but still very important. In fact, they may be more important today than ever before, because people have lower attention spans. People seem to get distracted easily, and that may deter any person away from achieving their goals.

It is easy to get distracted- I get distracted- a lot! The sound of a text notification or the popup on our devices sparks curiosity. Once I get that notification, I want to know. When I check a notification, it usually is nothing. I am sure that many of you reading this, have experienced this. These notifications are made to get our attention, and we easily give it quickly.

Now, I have many responsibilities to get work done. I am not exempt from everyday responsibilities. I have my family, my work, the church, and projects that I work on. If I do not hone it all in, I can lag behind. I can get easily distracted, so I have to make sure not to fall into that trap. With much going on in my own life, efforts must be made to set out time for things as much as possible.

What I personally have found to do, is to take certain buckets of time to work on specific tasks. If I am writing a song, I may take an hour chunk of time to work on that song. When this happens, I give it 100% mental energy. This is what I do personally. You may have a different way. Find your way that you get things done. I understand that what you may do may be different than what I do. I am merely sharing what I do. By taking certain blocks of time to do certain things, it allows for me to get in the state of flow, or to be in the zone, and get as much work done as possible. This has helped me stay on top of it all instead of falling behind.

When my son was a newborn and was asleep, I would have

to use all of my energy and effort to do as much work as I could. This actually is how I got started blocking out pieces of time. Yes, I admit, I was undisciplined. That was my vice. However, my son actually made me realize that I have to get more disciplined. So if I had 15 minutes, or an hour and a half, I would get as much work as I could have done without any distractions. This meant, no phone, no television, no computer, and no people. This has helped me enormously, and maybe this may help you.

I want to take a moment and briefly explain what caused me to begin on this journey. Working in corporate America was something that I thought was the best for me. I had heard so often that I needed to go to school, get a degree, and then find a stable job. This is something that many people are taught. Many people live this out. This way of doing life was exactly what I did. I distinctly remember right before I graduated with my bachelors in business management, I felt moved to start to apply to different companies for a position. I felt that I had arrived. I was ready to enter the next chapter of my life. I finally would be able to make it and be happy. So, I applied to a couple of places. I was ecstatic to be hired in the first place I applied. I felt lucky knowing this was uncommon. When I signed all the paperwork before starting on day one, I remember being told that this is the place to be. I remember how people were saying that some employees started at the bottom and made it to top management. This motivated me. That is what I wanted at the time. I believed in this idea that I would find happiness and fulfillment in this new season of life. I was happy, but only for a short time.

So what happened? What made me go leave this? Well, I believe that a lot of it had to do with me buying into the illusion. What is the illusion? Well, it is this idea that you are to live life a certain way, by doing certain things and fitting into the mold that culture teaches. Some people are meant to follow this framework of life. You know, go to school, get good grades, work in a career, get married, move to the suburbs, and live happily ever after. Then, after years of working, you get to retire and get your golden watch. Then you enjoy the remaining years of your life in retirement. I felt that this was the model that everyone should follow. I followed this without question and without really any thought. I certainly felt that I was doing things the "right" way.

When I began working at the company, I loved it. I loved the routine and I loved the people. I supported the work culture. I worked in an organization that I believed in. I believed in their vision and mission. I had felt that I had arrived. I internally believed at the time that I could work here for the rest of my life. I believed in this idea of success. I worked hard and I wanted to do everything within my power to be promoted up and then everything would be happily ever after.

I remember that my therapist used to tell me, "Who we are is a result of a series of events that occur…". These are true words, and I would soon discover that a series of events would occur that would push me to go onto this journey. If these events never occurred, this book that you are reading never would have been written. Even though these events were a transition for me, I am thankful. I am grateful that these events happened. These events led me to where I am today.

At that time, I was newly married. My wife and I lived in Orange County, one of the richest areas in the country. Living in Orange County came with a high cost of living. We both had to work. I had a new car. I had a new career path, and everything seemed to be set. We both felt at the time that we were taking the path most taken would lead us to make it. Making it to us, was being financially stable and living a life of happiness and fulfillment. We were wrong.

At first, I was happy. I enjoyed the job. Things began to change in the company culture though. Things also were changing in the church that we were attending. The church was and still is important. My wife and I have the heart to serve, and we love helping the local church. During that time, we were both employed part-time at this church. Over time, little changes made a big difference. The church we attended was going through a transition. The company I was working at also was going through a transition. Both of these changes were undesirable. The culture of the company that I was working for began to change. It was going through layoffs and restructuring. Subtle changes were happening during the time I was there, and I kept telling myself that everything would be okay. I also did the same thing at the church changes.

The most significant thing that was happening at the church and the company was a change of leadership. Leadership caused changes in culture. The leadership at both places decided to go into another direction. Leadership is of critical importance. When things change in your life, it can cause you to change. With external circumstances changing, I wanted to change as well. These events pushed me to change my situation, but also helped me begin a journey of internal change.

The church had changes in structure, theology, and styles. My wife and I made the conscious decision to leave the church. It was a hard decision, but one that was necessary. This decision was but a contribution to the search for fulfillment in my personal life. I write this not to bash, but to allow for you to be aware of where I once was. These events were a part of a series of events that led me to where I am today.

The company went through internal changes that allowed for people to no longer promote from within. Simply put, the very thing that I was told in the beginning, no longer mattered. I could no longer promote from within the company. Ouch! That was pretty much the indicator that I was no longer going to be there. One of my goals was to work up in a company. If promotion was impossible, I had no motivation to excel. Sadly, my position was becoming a dead-end job.

I was unhappy. I would talk to coworkers, trying to keep the happiest face possible. My coworkers would talk about how they have been doing the same things over and over for the past several years. I felt as though I was the odd man out. How could this be? Doesn't everyone want to be the best that they can be? Don't people want to grow and become all that they are made to be? These questions were in my mind. I wanted answers.

How could people allow for these changes and not do anything? For work, people just rolled with the punches. I remember a lot of my coworkers saying that they have to support these changes. They valued their job, not the loss of growth. For the church, people tried to enable positive change, but it was shut down. During this time, I learned many lessons.

I learned very quickly that some people who have no desire, no drive, no motivation to promote. Some people have the mindset that as long as they are stable, or remain as they are, they are set. I remember people telling me that as long as they still had a job, they would be fine. As for the church, the shift and changes in structure and culture were final. Nothing could be done.

I knew that I would eventually leave, but how? I began to plan with my wife. A transition from the city, to a smaller town, my hometown, seemed essential. So, in late 2017, I made this decision that I would begin a journey. I had questions that needed answers. It took the changes in the culture, the desire to change, and other small events that made me respond to it. I was ready for changes.

This realization alone contributed to my commitment to growth. I felt this drive to learn. I was in debt, unhappy, and wanted change. I was happy in my marriage and with my family. Other things though, needed change. I took a different path.

I remember when I was beginning my journey I dedicated much time to learning. I would listen to audiobooks, read, and take online courses. I knew that I wanted to change, and I knew that I would find answers. Why did I begin to do this? Well, it simply was because I was unhappy with the direction that my life was going in. I was in a lot of debt. I had racked up a ton of going to college. I wanted to end the cycle of more debt.

Keep in mind, I was unhappy with the debt, the changes in the job, and the changes in the church. Not only was I unhappy with these changes, I felt unfulfilled. I wanted to find meaning and purpose in my life. This decision would begin me on a new journey. I was unsure where this journey would take me, but I was okay with that. I was happy about being newly married. Sometimes, when a series of events happen in your life, it pushes you to change. Sometimes you are nudged to begin on a journey.

At the time, I was planning on getting my Masters in Business Administration at the college that I had originally got my bachelor's in. The cost for the Master's Degree would have cost $20,000. Even though this was a more affordable option, the fact that my wife and I had collected up a bunch of debt in a new marriage, was unwise. I look back at it all in regret. Being in so much debt is one of the only regrets I have in my own life. Knowing what I know now, I would have made sure that my wife and I only got our four-year degrees. Now, my wife is very happy with the master's degree that she got, but I just do wish that I was better at managing my money. I also want to say that I do not regret going to college. I regret the debt. I wish college was more affordable for people, but that is another discussion.

There exists an abundance of knowledge, wisdom, and information. It is out there! It excites me to see how much information is readily available. Commit to learning. Commit to growth. You can do this without getting into debt. It really breaks down to what you are reading, what you are putting into your mind and the heart behind it all. Reading is another important aspect to committing to growth. Reading can expand your mind greatly, and it is another way to discover new passions or learn more and build upon the one you are most drawn towards. In addition, courses, webinars, videos, and other content available to help you grow. Since late 2017, to this day, I still read, take courses, and listen to audiobooks. I do not plan to stop.

We should never stop learning. We should never stop growing. Just think of the massive amounts of information that is readily available. What an amazing opportunity that you can partake in. Even the wisdom from the Word of God is readily available. There exists a vast amount for you to choose from. Choose wisely.

Not only that, if we were to study for a short time, even just ten minutes, but that would also mean that you are studying for less than one percent of a given day! Wow. If you were to study for an hour and day, that would be a little over 4% of the 24-hour time period. Just a few minutes or an hour is a very small amount of time. If you disciple yourself to learn every day, you are sowing knowledge and wisdom into your life. Just imagine what you will reap. When you make a commitment to continue to learn and grow, implement what you learn into your life. You will see that small changes can make a huge difference in your own life. We do not always have to make big changes.

At the church that I serve at, the leadership constantly challenges young adults and teenagers to partake in a

10-minute reading challenge of the Word of God. I found it to be very interesting that reading for 10 minutes is less than 1% of your day. It goes to show you how much time we have in a day. It keeps me and others in check. It also makes you wonder how much time you waste.

If you are serious and passionate about discovering your purpose, it will not be a hassle to make time to commit to growing. See to it that you will do whatever it takes. Whatever means necessary that works for you such staying up later, waking up earlier, you will find your way. Persist. Persevere. You will make it.

Even back in 2017, I was learning so much via audiobooks, reading, studying, and taking online courses. I had this thirst in this hunger to obtain as much knowledge, wisdom, and information as possible. I did this to improve my life. I started this journey as a path for myself to grow. Over time, as I have grown, more desire to share what I have learned with others. That is actually the primary reason why I have written this book.

I encourage you. With everything that you learn and experience, you should be open to sharing it. You can empower and encourage people in their own way. Your life can have a very profound effect on people, even if it is just one person. Just imagine the possibilities of the impact you can have on other peoples. The impact can be one person or 1 million people. I do not think that this book will have that much of an impact on people, but I pray that this book will even help text one person improve their life a little bit.

You can begin your journey of development, growth, and

learning. Do this to become the best that you can be. This is part of going for your God-given potential. God desires for you to be the best you can be. Be encouraged to grow in relationship with God and in the pages of Scripture. For me personally, I believe that we should be encouraged to grow in knowledge and wisdom. Wisdom comes from Scripture. Knowledge comes from what we learn in the world.

Some people may view what you are doing as selfish, self-centered, or simply wrong. Remember, you can make a greater impact on the lives of other people. When I grow, learn, and study, I also implement those lessons in my life. Once the implementation occurs, it helps my life personally. From there, I can help spread knowledge, and wisdom to others. We are better when we help other people around us. We can truly make a difference in the lives of others when we help others reach their God-given potential.

When I talk about this idea of growth and Improvement, I mean this in so many different ways. I believe that we should always be on a path to becoming the best that we can be, even on a spiritual level. Since I began this project, I have been more and more interested in studying the pages of the Word of God. Not only am I studying ways to develop people, but I am studying line by line books of the Bible. I have found such joy in studying the Word of God and learning so many different subjects.

We only have one life to live, and so, why not take the time to begin on a journey to become the best that you can be.

7

Taking Responsibility

This chapter is a harder topic to talk about. As I have grown through this life, I have noticed something. Many people blame others for their problems. It is becoming more common for people to blame their problems on the government, individuals, events, and other factors. I do believe though, that although bad things can happen in your life, how you respond is what is critical. To take responsibility for life helps you understand past problems. To help move forward with bringing meaning in life, you need to learn how to take ownership of your life.

Before I started on this journey, I felt as though I was a victim. When an inconvenience would occur, I would blame everyone but myself. I would never take a step back and examine. Could I be the cause of this? Could I be reaping something that I have sowed? It took me this journey to understand that a lot of the problems that I ran into were by my own doing. So many times, I have reaped bad because I had sown bad.

Living in this culture, it is easy to get angry and blame others. Our culture teaches us to be angry, loud, arrogant, jealous at others. We react to the hardships that life throws at us. To react, that is different than to respond. Many people react instead of responding. To respond is to take time to think and consider before acting.

People get offended when other people do not agree with them. This can be politics, faith, and other topics. This is an example of humans reacting and not responding. People seem to get offended easily, instead of making efforts to understand the other side of the argument. We should strive to show love and compassion. I do not write these things to make a political statement. I write these things as a reminder to myself and others to be more understanding, compassionate, and loving. We should do these things towards people even if we do not agree with them. This can be a very hard thing to do at first. It takes practice to respond rather than to react. I may not agree with the things that you do, but I can and will treat you respectfully as a human being. I expect that with the people I interact with, they will do the same. The victim mindset is becoming more and more popular. People get offended easily. Our identity does not exist in how we are offended. Our identity exists in who and what we are. Our potential pushes us to respond.

It seems that most of these individuals do not take a step back to realize why a disagreement has happened. Also, why are offended? What, at the core, caused us to be triggered? Let us evaluate the heart of the matter. Some individuals choose to get their feelings hurt and to get offended and angry. To take your life to the next level and to become a better person you must start to understand others. We must take responsibility for our lives and how we act!

(John 15:12 HCSV) goes on to say "This is My command: Love one another as I have loved you." Can we not seek to come to understand one another, even if our opinions or views on life are different? We can surely stand firm on what we believe in even if we do not agree with another person. We can treat people respectfully and communicate. As a Christian, I follow what the Word of God says, and even though that may be counter-cultural, I still do everything that I can to be an example of what Christ would be. I also strive to meet as many people as possible and to hear their different perspectives. I stand firm on what I believe in, but that doesn't mean that I will not want to hear another perspective, and try to understand where people are coming from. We are all on a different journey.

How we respond to life is important. When hardships occur in our lives, we must think before we act. I am not saying that you should not feel. Feelings are natural. It is what you do with your emotions. It is how you go about your internal feelings. Take full ownership of your life. This is but a great way to be empowered.

Let us strive to remain in control of how we act to occurrences. We only can control ourselves, not any other human being. It is impossible to fully control someone else. You may wish to yell and scream for another to be different, but that is only doing an injustice. This is a very hard thing for anyone to accept. I wish I could change people, but that is impossible. I wish I could have forced people to choose something different, but I am powerless. What I can do, is be there for someone when they need me. This can be for advice or help. You certainly can try to persuade someone into the way that you see things, but that doesn't mean that they will believe. I say these things, as a matter of patience, you have to be patient with people, and try to help them improve as much as possible.

I also realize that people sometimes feel power over you after getting a rise out of you. When someone is yelling at you, calling you names, they want you to get angry. They crave for you to submit to them. The moment you lose your temper, the moment you lose control, they win. This is all a battle of emotions. It is your job to take full responsibility and control your emotions. Do not let others take control of you or your emotions. This is a very hard thing to do. I have met some people who will try to test my patience, and I have got to prove to myself and the other person that external words will not affect my internal emotions. How can you expect to change things for the better if you remain unaware and irresponsible of yourself?

To take responsibility for your life means that you are in full control of your emotions, and how you respond to any given situation. What someone does on the outside, is on them. What is on me, it was my decision. If someone tries to belittle me, I will not let them have control over me or my emotions. In the past, I gave people control over me. In reality, I am in control. This is a gift from God. God gives you your life and you can rise to respond to life.

This is part of taking ownership. God has created your life.

We can choose what life we want to live in. Be empowered. Ask yourself, do you want to let someone else control your happiness? Or do you want to take control of your emotions?

I have met so many people whose hope is in something that is fleeting. Sometimes people put their trust in petty things. I've met people where their entire lives are focused on other people. We can choose to live and thrive in our current state. We just have to take responsibility for our life. It is said that responsibility is our ability to respond. I pray that we may all take ownership and responsibility of our life. Let us come to realize that we are in control and that it is God who gives us this ability to take control of our own lives.

8

Having Vision

"Where there is no vision, the people perish"
(Proverbs 29:18 KJV)

What is your vision for your life? Where do you want to be? Who do you want to become? What life do you want to lead? There has always got to be a vision for what is most important to you in life. This vision will give you clarity for where you want to be. Without having a vision, we can become lost. If we are but lost in life, won't our life remain meaningless? To have a vision is to bring clarity. To bring clarity is to bring meaning to your life.

This can range from anything between relationships to business endeavors. There must always be a vision you picture for where you want to go. Without vision, you can lose sight of what it is you are putting all your energy towards. Let us not be a drifter. Let us not be someone lost in life.

This verse from Scripture is always an interesting one for me. In the context of proverbs, Solomon is talking about people who would perish without divine vision. We can also find that this can be applied to our everyday lives, business, and other things. Having a vision is a good thing to have. When we have a vision of where we want to be, we can make efforts to get there. We can even inspire and motivate people with a vision.

Sometimes the process of creating a vision of your life can be difficult. Some people want to have a perfect vision. It is better to have a vision rather than none at all. Over time, you can change the overall vision for your life. We are told from a young age to create big dreams. However, as we age, our big dreams turn into "unrealistic", deemed by all factors except ourselves. The media, peers, family, the culture all convince us that our dreams we were once told were to be larger than life are now a "waste of time". Hopefully, we are not like the coworker I once knew who gave up on all of her dreams. If you have, you can always think big again. Like a muscle, these things take practice.

I am here to tell you that your dreams are attainable, but it lies in your hands. You are fully capable of doing great things. Do not underestimate yourself. You are a creation from God. You were made in the image of God as mentioned in Genesis 1:27. God is the great creator, and I personally believe that God is filled with joy when we create. And so we should be empowered to create a vision for our life. Ask yourself, what is a dream or vision for where you want to be in life?

Envision yourself there. Imagine you have accomplished a goal, reached a dream, or that vision a reality. Picture it in your mind. Once you have it pictured in your mind, determine the steps you will take to reach that point, and begin to put those steps into effect. Sometimes you have to work from the end first. Sometimes you have a plan from the accomplishment back to the beginning. This depends on the situation or the person. What does a fulfilled life look like? What does happiness look like to you? Only you can answer these questions. It is up to you. It is your dream.

Take time to discover where it is you would like to be in life. Imagine it wholeheartedly. Envision the setting, the emotions, the colors, the sounds. Feel it in its rawest form. People may tell you never to dream. Ignore this. Aim high. Dream big. Once you unlock your God-given potential, the power is yours. To have a vision in your mind is the first step. Going out and doing it, that is the next step.

Ask, and it shall be given you; seek, and ye shall find; knock, and it shall be opened unto you (Matthew 7:7 KJV).

You can ask always God for guidance. I encourage you to do this. Sometimes we know where we are meant to go in life. Other times, we are unsure where to go in life. Ask God for where to go in this life. We can pray to God. We can open the Scriptures for guidance as well.

You can seek counsel. You can find people in your life who can support you, encourage you, and motivate you to move. Some people seek out people to keep them accountable. Consider such matters.

"Shoot for the moon. Even if you miss, you'll land among the stars." - Norman Vincent Peale

9

Strength

Live life as though nothing can stop you. Live life as though you have already accomplished what you have set out to do. (Philippians 4:13 NKJV) goes on to say "I can do all things through Christ who strengthens me." I have always found this verse to be encouraging. When you know the Lord, you seek him out, and it is Christ who gives you strength. That strength that comes from within much can be accomplished. Strength will help you persist when you go on your journey. We have got to persevere when we are searching for meaning in life. Let us never go backward.

It is okay to ask God for strength and to find the confidence that comes through him. I have found that in my relationship with God, I have confidence, strength, joy, and peace that comes from him. I no longer I'm afraid of people. I am not longer afraid of situations that come my way. I put my trust in God.

Think about individuals who have reached the goal that you are working towards. Examine how they act and incorporate that into your life. This is known as mirroring. Analyze successful people and see how you can adapt. Please remain authentic in doing this. Remain genuine in how you talk, how you sound, how you act. It all matters. I'm not saying to become a whole new person, rather incorporate these habits. Find what works for you. Find what you can improve on from others. That is what makes us all unique. We put our own spin on things, as we are all different works of God's creation.

I took a class a few years back where I had to interview someone successful. I interviewed the CEO of a multi-million dollar company. What I learned, was golden. I learned about empowerment and allowing people to work together. I learned how you need to put into people. Interestingly to me, he indirectly talked about sowing and reaping. Sow into your people, you will reap a great culture of people. From that interview, I found things that I could implement in my own life. Now, I do not run a company, but I still learned a lot. I love what (Proverbs 15:22 NIV) goes on to say about this "Plans fail for lack of counsel, but with many advisers they succeed." Essentially I sought out counsel. I met up with this man a few times, and he gave me some great advice. Just as the verse suggests, with advisers, they succeed. Something that you can implement into your life, is finding people who can counsel you, advise you, or help you on your path.

Life can change drastically after you have reached your goal. Many people say money is the root of all evil. Who you are at your core will become magnified. Become a person of integrity. Be a person of character. Do these things. Strive for fulfillment. Seek God. Become who you are meant to be. Become more.

I have found that as I have grown, there will always be unhappy people. People will try to bring you down. People will try to derail or distract you. Be aware. Be alert. Keep moving toward reaching your potential. You were born with a purpose.

This is where it is of critical importance to become a person of character, and a person of God. If I am someone who steals before I am wealthy, I will most likely steal when I am wealthy. We should be encouraged to become people who have a good moral compass. Let us know what is right and what is wrong. Unfortunately, in our culture, many people believe that right or wrong does not exist. I personally turn to the pages of the Word of God. It has helped me develop holistically as a person.

I encourage you to become an authentic person. Become real and not fake. People can tell if you are being genuine or not. Be warm, friendly, and the person people want to be around. Exhibit love. Show kindness. Listen. Learn. Love. Become the man or the woman of God has intended you to be. I believe that you have a great amount of potential within you.

10

Everything in Excellence

Many paths exist that you can take in the journey of life. It is easy to become overwhelmed by so many options. In all that you do, I implore you to seek God out. Allow God to help you become into the person you are meant to be. I believe that because God has designed you, and given you potential, you should seek him out. Pursue God. God will help lead and guide you. We can seek him out through prayer, through a relationship, and through the Word of God. What better way to have meaning in your life than to do everything in excellence? Be proud of what you do and how you did it.

With the endless opportunities of what you can become, take some time to try new things, or revisit old interests. Discover yourself. You may be surprised by what you uncover. It is okay to try things and fail in the beginning. Say you decide to take up painting. You may not be so great at it upon trying, but you truly enjoy it. Do not allow your novice level to push you away from continuing if you are passionate about it. Keep painting and grow your skills. You can become great at anything if you dedicate your time to it.

Whatever you end up discovering, do them as good as possible. Whatever it is that you are pursuing, give it all you got. Do the best you can. Do not be discouraged. With time and dedication, you will become amazing.

Excellence should not be confused with perfection. Perfection is unattainable. Remove that concept of perfection out of your brain. Perfection exists only in God. Human beings are imperfect beings. We can work hard to become amazing. We will never reach perfection.

You may not be able to become perfect, but you can become outstanding at anything if you dedicate your time and energy to it. Some may be born with innate passion and developed it earlier in life, others may find it later. Regardless, what they share in common is that they dedicate their time to it. Persistence and patience are prerequisites to become and remain great. Continue to put in the work in and become better.

Give your all to whatever it is that you discover is your passion. You can become astounding if you work at it. Excellence means to give it all you got in that given moment. As you progress, you will give even more and more if you do it in excellence. The journey never ends because perfection does not exist. You can always become greater than the last time.

I tell many people that in everything we do, we do in excellence for the glory of God. This is something that I live by. This is something that I strive for. This is something that I desire for everyone to implement into their lives. We should do everything in excellence, and not just do the bare minimum. I believe that so many people do the bare minimum in everything, and their lives show it. It is so much better to be able to finish a task and say to yourself that you did the best you could. That's how I want to live my life. I want to live my life to the best of my ability, and I encourage you to live the life that God has given to you to the best of your ability. You only have one life to live here on the earth, so let's make the best of this life.

11

Love

Lead with love in every aspect of your life. Love means to live authenticity. To live with love means to be genuine. Be real with yourself. To contradict this is only doing a disservice to yourself. You may feel comfortable within a false identity or construct of your current life situation, but you will only grow if you begin to live in truth. Be real with others as well. People are able to sense when you are being fake. You do not have to put up a front in any direction you choose to take. People will appreciate your sincerity and this will only add positively to your situation. Live in truth. When we live in truth, we can fully love. It is said that the truth will set you free. Be real, be free. Love will bring forth meaning to your life. Love will bring you joy.

With whichever route you choose to take, you must always love yourself every step of the way. Even when you are struggling, love that version of you. God created you with love. He designed you for a purpose. God wants you to discover and fulfill your potential. It is easy to compare yourself to others who have already reached success. However, you must remember we each have been made to bring something different to the world. We are all made unique. This is why you should not beat yourself down over feeling less adequate than another individual. Everyone has their own story and was made to be one of a kind.

Something that I personally live by, is the idea that I should love God and love people. Part of doing this is to love and accept me. Because I am made in the image of God, I need to realize that I was made by God for more than the superficial. I was made for more. You were made for more.

It will be difficult to do so at times, but always try your best to stick to it, especially through the rough times in life. It takes some individuals time to love. Never stop loving. Love can rescue in times of turbulence. God is love. Love is beautiful.

Each of us was created with love by God. We are all different from one another and have our own special purpose on Earth. Nothing comes from comparing yourself to others and thinking poorly of yourself. Learn from others. Do not put others down. Love yourself and share this love with it to the world. Love comes from God, and it can flow through us.

I would like to share one of my favorite verses.

"If I speak in the tongues of men or of angels, but do not have love, I am only a resounding gong or a clanging cymbal. If I have the gift of prophecy and can fathom all mysteries and all knowledge, and if I have a faith that can move mountains, but do not have love, I am nothing. If I give all I possess to the poor and give over my body to hardship that I may boast, but do not have love, I gain nothing." (1 Corinthians 13:1-3 NIV)

This verse is significant. We can attain all of the success in the world. We can have material possessions. We can have all the knowledge, and we can become best in the world, but if we do not have love we are nothing. This verse keeps me in check. I hope that the verse is very thought-provoking for you. In all that we do, we certainly are to do in excellence. We also have to realize that we have got to have love in our hearts. We've got to implement love into our thinking and in our doing. We've got intimate love in our being and in our doing. Love is so important, and since God is love, we have got to live out our lives like God. We certainly will never be God, but we can become but examples of this love.

Light in the Darkness

As you continue to walk your journey, it is important to remember that you are to be a light in the darkness. We are all brought into a world that is broken. Life on Earth consists of constant struggles with disease, crime, and hatred. It is up to us, it is up to you, to go out and make a difference. Will you step out on this journey? Many people find meaning by inspiring others. A meaningful life is like a light that is radiant for others to see. Shine bright. Bring meaning to others as you seek out meaning to your life.

To make a difference, you must ensure you are becoming a person who others will be in admiration of. In other words, be an example for others to see. Live your life in such a way that people will look up to you. Don't be fake and do this, but be real, and do the right thing. Be a leader. Be empowered to step up. I want to be someone that people will look up to.

Be an inspiration to the people. Be a light that shines bright in the darkness of this world. To be light means to follow in God's example.

I want to share a few Bible verses with you as we are near

the end of this book. I truly hope that you have enjoyed reading so far.

In (1 John 1:5 NCV), it goes on to say in Scripture that "God is light, and in him there is no darkness at all." And this first gets me every single time. I want to come to the light instead of living a life that is in the darkness. I want to be someone who does good, rather than someone who does evil. I want to live a life that is wise, rather than living the life of a fool. It is my hope and it is my desire that you have the same or similar goals. I also think of the sun, and how it shines to sustain life. All life forms pretty much required, and without the sun, there would be no life. And since the sun gives off light, it is life-giving. I desired to come to the light, for the light is life-giving. And since God is light, I desire to pursue the path of life.

(John 8:12 ESV) "Again Jesus spoke to them, saying, 'I am the light of the world. Whoever follows me will not walk in darkness, but will have the light of life.'" One of the greatest decisions that you can make for yourself, is entering a relationship with the Lord Jesus Christ. As part of my journey, I studied many different subjects. I studied metaphysics, I studied body language, leadership, spirituality, science, and human potential. In all that I have studied, it actually led me to grow further in my love for God, Jesus Christ, and the Bible. I have found much wisdom in the Word of God. This wisdom has helped transform my life. Because God is light, we are to pursue the light. In pursuing the light and coming to God, we too can shine bright for many. I'm a firm believer that God empowers us to reach our God-given potential. Our light can shine so bright that people will take notice, and they will be inspired. People need to be encouraged and empowered to reach their God-given potential. With so much negativity on evil in this world, I believe that God desires for us to do good in this world.

(Matthew 5:14-16 CEB) "You are the light of the world. A city on top of a hill can't be hidden. Neither do people light a lamp and put it under a basket. Instead, they put it on top of a lampstand, and it shines on all who are in the house. In the same way, let your light shine before people, so they can see the good things you do and praise your Father who is in heaven." This verse also gets me so much. I desire to live my life for the glory of God. I truly desire to make a difference in this world, no matter how big or how small. Come to know the Lord. Pursue the deeper things of God. In doing this, you will find that you will light up like a beacon of hope and I encourage you to be that beacon of hope. The world needs people to do great things. And throughout the entire Bible repeatedly, we find in the pages of Scripture, God uses ordinary people to do extraordinary things.

By pursuing who you truly are, by unlocking your potential, you are coming into light. You are becoming the light as you are coming into the truth. You are being set free from the deceit, illusions, and the lies of culture. I pray that you may become aware, that you may come to learn the truth, but you will come to light, and that we will find life. Christ himself said in (John 14:6 NIV) "Jesus answered, 'I am the way and the truth and the life. No one comes to the Father except through me.'"

A great quality to possess as an inspiration is to be a learner. Never stop learning! To learn means to grow and develop. When you do this, you will come across wisdom. Wisdom is important and necessary. The simplicity of wisdom is transcendent through time and through the ages. I highly encourage you to study wisdom literature. Study the writings of Proverbs, and Ecclesiastes. Be challenged. I highly encourage that you seek these things out. When I have studied these books, I have been so challenged. Wisdom literature will help you grow because wisdom is part of the deeper things of God.

Nuggets of wisdom can be applied to any part of one's life. Be that a five-year-old or a 50-year-old. Wisdom is beautiful. Wisdom never fails. Wisdom must be shared. It is up to us to find and discover wisdom and truth, and it is up to us to share what we learn. We must share wisdom, knowledge, and truth with others. We can make a greater impact on this world.

When you seek out God and believe, you will achieve greater things. By seeking out God, and pursuing the path He laid for you, you will discover that each of us, including you, has been placed here for a purpose. Seek God and you will see you are meant to be greater and do greater.

Truly, truly, I say to you, whoever believes in me will also do the works that I do; and greater works than these will he do, because I am going to the Father.
(John 14:12 ESV)

We were made for more, for a greater purpose. It is up to us to find that purpose. Although we have a limited time, we have the potential to live a fulfilled life full of meaning and purpose.

You are made for more.

Concluding Thoughts

I want to thank you for taking the time to read this book. I want to take a moment and give you a brief recap of what we went over, as simply as possible.

We are given time, life, abilities and talents, and potential. These things are a gift from God. Within us, is a choice of what we are to do in this life on earth. The problem with so many people is that they waste themselves away by meaningless pursuits, it is merely chasing the wind. Within you is potential, and I encourage you to live life as good as possible. Consider your thoughts, for they make you who you are. Consider what you sow into your life, for you will reap. Take ownership and responsibility for your life. God empowers you to be the best version of yourself. God takes care of the big picture stuff, all you need to do is take charge of your life. Be responsible for your life by knowing that where you are is from a series of choices and events. Respond to life, instead of reacting. Have an overall vision for your life. Really take time and think of where you want to be. Once you have that vision, see to it that you take steps towards that vision. Be strong, persist, and persevere. No matter what people say or what people do to you, only you can make the final decision. God gives you the tools to venture out into the world, so remain firm. Strength comes from within, and when we falter and fail, we can always seek God, for God is the foundation, the ultimate strength. In all that you do, do in excellence for the glory of God. Do your best in this life. You have one life to life. As you live and as you grow, continue to love. Love God, love others, and love who you are. God loves you, so you to should learn to accept who you are. In all these things, be a light that shines in the darkness. This world is dark, broken, and lost. God empowers you to be a light in the darkness. God is light, love, life, and truth. By seeking God and being empowered, we can venture out. Be encouraged to lead, inspire, motivate, and empower others as well. Bring people to light.

You are made for more.

Patrick Dailey is Worship and Youth Director at Impact Christian Church in Victorville, California. He lives by the concept that "In everything you do, do in excellence for the glory of God". His hobbies include songwriting, hiking, driving, riding horses, and enjoys God's beauty.

Patrick is happily married to his wife, Amber Dailey. They have their newborn son, Aaron Dailey. Patrick and Amber Dailey enjoy serving in the local church, spending time in nature, quality time with family, and working together on projects.

www.ingramcontent.com/pod-product-compliance
Lightning Source LLC
Chambersburg PA
CBHW031312060726
47590CB00003B/1182